Osage County Quilt Factory

Overbrook, Kansas USA

Virginia Robertson

That Patchwork Place ®

Credits

Editor ....Barbara Weiland
Copy Editor ....Liz McGehee
Text and Cover Design....................Kay Green
Photography ....Brian Kaplan
                                              Judith Lennox-Hopson
Illustration/Graphics ....Nicki Salvin-Wight

Osage County Quilt Factory ©
©1992 by Virginia Robertson

That Patchwork Place, Inc.
PO Box 118
Bothell WA 98041-0118

Printed in the British Crown Colony of Hong Kong
97 96 95 94 93 92   6 5 4 3 2 1

Robertson, Virginia,
        Osage County Quilt Factory / Virginia Robertson.
            p.   cm. — (Quilt shop series)
        ISBN 1-56477-013-3 :
                1. Patchwork—Patterns. 2. Patchwork quilts.
        3. Osage County Quilt Factory (Osage County, Kan.)
        I. Title. II. Series.
TT835.R615 1992
746.9'7—dc20   92-13119
                                                      CIP

Acknowledgments

I wish to express my sincere appreciation
to those special people who have helped me
throughout the adventure of putting this
book together. Basically, these quilts were an
Osage County Quilt Factory staff effort. They
were discussed and analyzed by the employ-
ees. Not only did the staff members work on
quilts, but they also continued to do the day-
to-day responsibilities that keep the wheels
turning at the Quilt Factory. I appreciate the
contribution from each of them. My thanks
to Geri Cummings, Helen Crook, Meridee
Graham, Carolyn Meerian, Carol Simmons,
Doris Uhl, Grace Vaughn, and Amy Crook.

Special thanks go to Roxane Fawl, who
continues to decipher my cryptic notes and
manages to make some sense of them when
she commits them to the computer. Also,
thanks to Eva Hudson, whose sewing experience and drafting abilities are indispensable.

Thanks to my husband and business man-
ager, Lynn, who keeps the whole place running, from the computers to the lights in the
bell tower.

Special acknowledgments go to Judith
Lennox-Hopson for her writing contributions
and her wonderful photographic tour of the
shop.

Contents

The Quilt Factory Story

*The Osage County Quilt Factory
in Overbrook, Kansas*

At a recent Quilt Festival, two quilters were talking about the Quilt Factory. The first quilter was encouraging her friend to make the trip to see the place for herself. "It is a quilter's dream come true. Just imagine walking into church and having all the pews filled with wonderful fabric!"

On the outside, the 102-year-old building that houses the Osage County Quilt Factory still resembles a church. But on the inside . . . well, a few changes have been made to create one of the largest quilt shops in the Midwest. The pews have been replaced with fabric holders (even though they still look a little

The magic begins when you enter the Quilt Factory.

like pews) and the Sunday school classrooms now hold books, patterns, and notions. The pastor's office houses the business operation, and the choir rehearsal room is the shipping department. Ah, but fellowship hall still remains the same because now quilters gather there to learn how to quilt and to hold guild meetings. Every nook and cranny is filled with the fun and excitement of quilting.

First-time visitors often begin their conversations in quiet tones until they get past the foyer. As the quilters climb the stairs, an explosion of patterns, samples, and fabrics tells the story that this is no longer a church building but definitely a quilt shop. Entering the doorway leading into the store, customers are greeted with a friendly "Hello" from one of the sales staff and encouraged to browse to their heart's content. Fabric is everywhere, just beckoning the quilter to come on in and have a good time. Samples of the newest quilt and doll patterns are on display throughout the store so that the customer can see what is available and how it is made. Patterns line every wall, and if we don't have what you want, we can probably get it for you. The stage area is set aside for special displays of quilts, cloth dolls, or something new and exciting. Each area of the store is organized with specific items so the customer can find exactly the right thing in one place. Workshop students especially enjoy the organization, since that means they can run in and out of the store quickly during a class. Some customers have suggested that it might take more than one visit to see and appreciate everything we have to offer!

"Ecology Santa" and "Starstruck Quilt" are samples of "What's New."

Over the last few years, this safe old building has provided a rendezvous for quilters from all over the United States and many foreign countries, even though Overbrook, Kansas, seems like an unlikely place for such a quilt shop. The leisurely drive through the Kansas countryside to the Quilt Factory hardly prepares the shopper or student for what lies ahead.

Quilting no longer is a necessity but rather an adventure in creativity, whether it is for decorating or practical purposes. The Osage County Quilt Factory fosters this belief by offering as many classes as possible, covering all levels of quilting expertise. The most popular class continues to be the Block-of-the-Month Quilt.

Originally, the Block-of-the-Month classes were offered in response to so many requests from people who just wanted to learn how to quilt. A pattern was designed especially for the class. Most basic techniques for piecing and appliqué were covered during that year of discovery. Each block of the quilt represented a new month and a new technique. Since then, the original class has been repeated numerous times, and out of those classes have come five more patterns that could be taught using the concept of making one block each month. It's fun and it works. Students are thrilled with the successful completion of their finished quilts.

When a new pattern is developed, it is also important to introduce current products as well as new sewing techniques. By combining the latest skills and tools with the traditional patterns, today's quilter has many more options from which to choose. The "Kansas Sampler" is a favorite because the student also becomes the designer. The skill is mastered by doing several blocks in a single technique. When the blocks are completed, they are combined according to the ideas of the quilter. It is amazing to see the number of variations from a single class. Each top is unique.

The Osage County Quilt Factory is more than a building. It is about people expressing their creativity by learning to quilt. It is about wonderful fabrics, exciting colors, different techniques, trying out ideas, and having someone who appreciates those efforts to share in that experience.

Welcome to the store.

How to Use This Book

This book is divided into four basic sections. In the first section, "The Kansas Sampler," you will make a variety of quilt blocks and learn new skills with each one. Included are lessons on fabric and color selection, a list of the notions you'll need for quilting projects, how to prepare the fabric and cut the pieces, and finally, how to piece and press your blocks. After you complete your blocks, you'll learn how to design your own quilt top, using your sampler blocks, and how to complete it by adding batting, backing, and binding. All of the techniques in "Let's Make a Quilt!" can be applied to other blocks and quilts you make in the future.

Once you've learned the basics and completed your quilt, you can progress to the last two sections. "Kansas Sampler Quilts" includes directions for four sampler quilts that require blocks like those you learned to make in the first part of the book. Like the sampler quilts, the "Spin-Off Quilts" that follow are made using the basic techniques included with the directions for each of the blocks in the "Kansas Sampler," so it is important to absorb all the basic information first.

The grid sheets stapled in the center of this book are meant to be used for making half-square triangle blocks (page 21). If you need more grid sheets, write to the Quilt Factory for ordering information: Osage County Quilt Factory, 400 Walnut Street, Overbrook, Kansas 66524. Remember to order the grid sheets by the desired finished size for the blocks you are making.

The Kansas Sampler Blocks

The "Kansas Sampler" is a Block-of-the-Month quilt, designed to teach you patchwork, appliqué, and quilting methods that can be adapted to a variety of other quilt projects. Included are techniques for fast, contemporary quiltmaking as well as the more traditional methods. The quilt you will create with your blocks is a "process" quilt. That is, the quilt is designed as you sew—fabrics are added and deleted during the sewing/designing process. Beginning students feel comfortable because there is no preconceived, preplanned vision of the finished piece. It is a growing, flexible quilt; constant decision making occurs during the sewing. The amazing part is that by using this free-flowing method, you will actually learn how to plan and complete a quilt.

The key to having fun while creating any quilt top is not to be too rigid. By keeping an open mind and a positive attitude during the process, you will continue to grow—quilting will never become boring!

Classroom space provides a perfect work area for new quilts in the making.

The blocks in the quilt measure 12" finished (cut 12½" square to include seam allowances). All seams are ¼" wide. Make the number of each block indicated with the instructions for each, knowing that you may want to add more blocks later for a larger quilt. Remember, it is okay to add and delete fabrics and blocks as you create. Stay flexible and open to new quilting experiences—you'll learn more and have more fun.

Some of the sampler blocks require full-size templates for cutting the patches. Template patterns are included in the book so you can make permanent ones from template plastic. For detailed template-making instructions, see page 16.

Below is a list of the blocks you will make and the basic techniques and skills you will learn with each one. Have fun as you make these blocks to create your own one-of-a-kind Kansas Sampler.

The "Kansas Sampler with Piano Key Border" (also shown on page 48) is just one example of the many quilt variations possible using sampler blocks.

Quick Ninepatch (page 12)

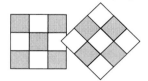

Strip Piecing
Chain Piecing
Pressing for Opposing Seams

Eight-Pointed Star (page 14)

Making and Using Templates
Hand Piecing

Half-Square Triangles (page 18)

Marking a Stitching Grid
Using Grid Sheets

Log Cabins (page 22)

Log Cabin Chain Piecing
String Blocks
Piecing on a Paper Foundation

Dresden Plate (page 30)

 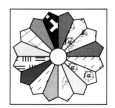

Hand Appliqué
Making Perfect Circles

Grandmother's Fan (page 32)

Curved Piecing

Crazy Quilt (page 34)

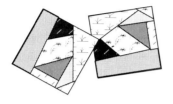

Random Piecing on a Paper Foundation

Color and Fabric Selection

Choosing is fun when it all looks so pretty.

The color in a quilt creates a mood or feeling. We perceive colors in so many ways. Some colors are clear. That is, they are pure, with no black, white, or any other color added. Other colors are muted. They can be tints, shades, or tones of the pure colors.

Pure colors are often described as bold, crisp, vivid, bright, or dramatic. Often, colors can be intensified by their placement. A pure color next to black or white becomes striking.

Muted colors include a lot of variations that can be confusing to match in quilts. Adding white to a pure color creates a pastel or a tint. Adding black to a pure color softens it to become a shade darker than the original color. If gray is added to a pure color, it becomes a tone of the original color. For example, country colors like dusty blues, mauves, buttery yellows, and gray-greens are tones of the original color.

Sometimes the print interferes with the perception of color, as in the case of the busy print or a fabric that includes lots of different colors. Stripes and plaids need special consideration when planning a quilt.

Aged fabrics have a special charm. The tea-dyed look involves overdyeing fabrics with tan dye or tea to create an aged look. Over-dyeing can also rescue busy fabrics that are otherwise too dominating to put in a quilt. Another way to create a subtle look is to simply turn the fabric over and use the back side.

Color choice is a very personal thing and should be approached with as much self-awareness as possible when choosing fabrics for a quilt. Many quilters are already in tune with the colors that feel right to them. They know exactly what colors they like to wear. Their homes are probably decorated in those same color families.

Fabric Requirements for Sampler Blocks

To make the blocks for your Kansas Sampler quilt, collect one-yard cuts of three different light-, three different medium-, and three different dark-colored fabrics. Use a variety of coordinating prints such as large prints, small prints, and plaids. Even some solids are okay. Choose an accent color that brings life and zip into the selection. Purchase ½ yard of this fabric, which I often call a "popper" color.

Note: For a king-size quilt, buy ½ yard extra of all the fabrics.

Choose the lattices or borders for the quilt after the blocks are finished. Feel free to add more fabrics for a "charm" or "scrap" effect in your quilt.

Helpful Hints

If you have no experience picking out and coordinating fabrics, consider the following methods to give you some direction.

- Choose a fabric with lots of different colors in the print. Using that fabric as a guide, begin to select your colors. Actually, the fabric designer has done all the work, and you can have all the fun. Don't be afraid to experiment. Sometimes a small amount of an unusual fabric can make a big difference in the final outcome of your quilt.

- For a contemporary look, start with a colorful plaid, a Madras perhaps. Select solid colors, using the plaid as the starting place. Remember, you can expand a color by selecting darker or lighter shades within the same color family. Notice the amount of each color in the plaid in relation to surrounding colors.

- When a quilt "glows" or has a color gradation from light to dark, the luminous effect is achieved by blending fabrics. Begin the block by selecting one very dark and one very light fabric. Gradually add medium colors in subtle tonal changes. These fill-in colors hold things together and create interest.

- Keep the color selection very simple. Use only shades of one color such as light, medium, and dark blue. This is called a monochromatic color scheme. Don't worry. The variety of prints within each color choice will keep things from being boring. The "Quilter's Thimble Sampler" on page 51 is an example of a quilt done in a monochromatic color scheme.

Selection Summary

1. Use a wide range of fabrics, colors, and textures to create interest.
2. Try different values to suggest design, contrast, and dimension.
3. To create luminosity, integrate fabrics with subtle value changes.
4. Select a "blender" fabric, one with lots of colors in the print to unify all the colors in the quilt.
5. An accent or "popper" fabric adds sparkle and can make the design "pop"

Even the fabric selections glow when they are placed in the store.

when used sparingly. Too much of a popper will overpower or dominate the color scheme.
6. Using colors in proportion maintains the feel or color theme of the quilt.
7. Busy fabrics tend to dominate other prints and colors, so use sparingly or in contrast with a calmer fabric surface.
8. Using stripes, plaids, or geometrics can create a sense of movement or direction.
9. The basic hues on a color wheel are a good way to organize color on the shelf or in a quilt.
10. Boring fabrics can be used effectively in a quilt, either to give contrast, or to create a resting place for the eye. Solid- or neutral-colored fabrics can highlight favorite fabrics. Fabrics you consider "ugly" by themselves might work well in a quilt when cut into small patches.
11. Color and texture choice in fabric is personal. Do what feels right for you, rather than what you "think" others approve of in quilts.
12. The bright, vivid, pure colors on the color wheel tend to coordinate in a project as do tints, shades, or tones. Avoid grayed tones with pure colors.
13. Warm colors advance and seem larger, while cool colors recede and appear smaller.
14. Pure, vivid colors advance, while tones, tints, and shades recede.

A quiet, sunny corner contains the latest in quilt books.

Necessary Notions

Here is a list of the most-used quilting supplies to help you get started. You may find you want to add to these tools as your personal style of quilting evolves.

- Good, sharp, fabric-cutting scissors
- Another pair of scissors for cutting paper, lightweight cardboard, and template plastic
- A rotary cutter, mat, and an ⅛"-thick clear acrylic ruler for rotary cutting
- A cardboard cutting board with 1" grid lines (not dots), only if you do not wish to use the rotary cutter
- Super-fine, glass-headed pins
- Long, flat-headed pins for use with a rotary cutter
- A suction-cup handle for holding and lifting rotary-cutting rulers easily
- Washable, soft-lead pencil
- Quilter's silver marking pencil
- Fabric eraser
- Two sheets of template plastic, 11" x 17"
- Size #1 or #2 quilter's safety pins—stainless steel so they don't rust
- Ecru or neutral-colored cotton sewing thread for piecing

- Quilting thread
- Fine thread (machine embroidery) for appliqué
- Package of quilting needles (Betweens) in sizes 8–12 (the larger the number, the smaller the needle)
- Size 11 or 12 Sharps for appliqué
- Thimble that fits middle finger on sewing hand
- Clear, acrylic ruler with ¹⁄₁₆" markings
- Fabric glue stick
- Fine seam ripper (Seam rippers get dull with use, so buy a new one after several years of heavy use.)
- Large darning needle for making seam-allowance holes in template plastic

Fabric Preparation and Cutting

Prewash all fabrics in warm water before using. Be sure to unfold the fabric so the center crease is open. Cotton and cotton blends may be combined in a single project if all the fabrics have been preshrunk. Many quilters prefer to use only 100% cotton fabrics, adding blends only when the color is just right for the project.

Prewashing removes the sizing and softens the fabric for easier hand quilting. Wash small pieces by hand, using a few drops of mild detergent. Rinse until the water is clear. To discourage raveling, drip dry and press rather than using the clothes dryer.

To find the straight of grain, tear one cut edge (if it wasn't torn in the store when you purchased it) to use as a guide for cutting. If you are using a printed check or geometric design and find that it is printed off-grain, you may use the fabric on the bias instead. Sometimes, only the edges are off-grain and the fabric toward the center is usable.

Keeping your scissors sharp is extremely important. If the scissors are not sharp, they will twist the fabric as they cut, causing inaccurate sizes and lots of piecing problems later.

Rotary cutters are a wonderful tool for maintaining accuracy while cutting several layers of fabric at one time. Check to be sure you are getting clean cuts. If there are a few uncut threads, it may be time for a new blade.

To prepare for cutting, fold the fabric in

half with selvage edges matching and place it on the rotary-cutting mat. Using the mat greatly reduces the chance of nicking the cutting blade and protects the table or other surface underneath from cuts and scratches. Roll the blade away from the body when cutting. For best results, use a ruler especially designed for rotary cutting. It should be at least ⅛" thick and at least 1" longer than the piece being cut. If the ruler is too short for a clean follow-through, fold the fabric in half again and cut. It is easy to cut through four layers of fabric with a good, sharp rotary cutter.

For additional information on using the rotary cutter, see *Shortcuts* by Donna Lynn Thomas (That Patchwork Place, Inc.).

Stitching and Pressing

Accurate piecing and careful pressing are critical to the success of any quilting project. As you make the sampler blocks, you will learn to piece by hand and by machine. You are free to choose the method you prefer after you've tried both.

With either method, it is very important to maintain a consistent ¼"-wide seam when stitching. For hand piecing, you can mark stitching lines on the wrong side of the patches with a lead or silver marking pencil.

To maintain a consistent ¼"-wide seam on the sewing machine, measure with the needle down and put masking tape to the right of the presser foot on the sewing-machine platform or guide plate. Then you can sew straight, even seams without working too hard to see the seam guide.

Use a good cotton thread in a matching or neutral color for piecing. Never use stretchy, fuzzy thread. If your machine needle "thunks," it is dull. Replace the needle after four hours of hard sewing, such as zigzag stitching or machine embroidery, or after a total of eight hours of normal sewing.

If your machine is sewing improperly, replace the needle, wind a new bobbin (under tension, so it doesn't become lumpy), and rethread the machine from the beginning. If none of this fixes the problem and all else fails, read the instruction manual, or call your friendly repairman!

When sewing, try not to pull or push the fabric through the machine. Let the feed dog do the work. If there is weight on one end, lift the fabric level with the feed dog. It is not necessary to backstitch when sewing patchwork, if the stitch length is shorter than you would normally use for regular sewing. Set the machine for 18 to 20 stitches per inch. Also, sewing a few stitches beyond the edge of the patches, creating a thread chain, will help keep the stitching from coming undone. Stitches will stay put if patchwork is not stretched during the pressing and sewing.

Remember, fabric is a flexible, moving, changing medium. It can be curved, twisted, flattened, and manipulated into almost any shape. Be aware of all its properties and respect the fabric in order to get it to do what you want. If you poke it with the point of a hot steam iron, don't be surprised if it has a distorted "pooch" or sagging seam line. Gently and firmly press with a medium setting on the iron and a light mist of steam, keeping everything flat and even. An ironing board cover with a grid really helps keep the pressing straight. Press, don't iron. Quilts are flat, not the shaped-in-the-round contours created in clothing construction.

Whenever possible, press patchwork seams to one side for greater strength and easier quilting. Press seams away from light fabrics, so the dark seams won't show through. If you plan to press seams open, be sure to use a shorter stitch length when sewing. Try not to make mistakes, because shorter stitches are more difficult to rip out!

To avoid stretching the fabric when ripping out a seam, pick and break every fourth or fifth stitch from the top with a very fine seam ripper. Pull loose with the bottom thread. Press and steam the fabric back into shape before sewing again.

The Sampler Blocks

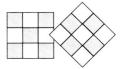

Quick Ninepatch Blocks

For your Ninepatch blocks, choose a very light and a very dark fabric. High contrast is desired for this block. Also, try to pick prints in two different scales, such as a tiny calico with a medium vine, and a large floral in a quiet monochromatic, tone-on-tone color scheme. Choose interesting fabrics for these blocks, because the patches are large.

Directions
Make four Quick Ninepatch Blocks.
1. Cut 3 strips, each 4½" x 27", from the light-colored fabric. Cut 3 strips, each 4½" x 27", from the dark-colored fabric.

Note: If the strips are cut 4½" x 44" (across the width of the fabric), you can make 6 Ninepatch blocks, with some pieced scraps left over to save for the Crazy Quilt Blocks (page 34).

2. Sew 2 light strips to 1 dark strip, with the dark strip in the center. Use ¼"-wide seams. Press seams toward the dark strip.

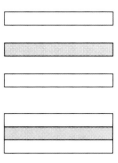

3. Sew 2 dark strips to 1 light strip, with the light strip in the center. Press the seams toward the dark strips. Measure across the striped units to be sure they measure 12½" across. If they do not, rip out and resew.

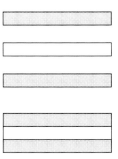

4. Using an acrylic ruler and rotary cutter, cut away selvages at the ends of each strip-pieced unit.

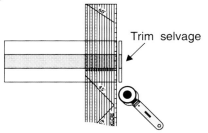

Trim selvage

5. Cut across the strip-pieced units every 4½".

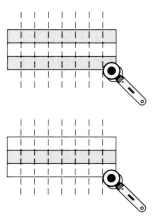

6. Assemble the Ninepatch blocks as shown. Pin with seams opposing so they don't slip during sewing. Press the seams toward the dark side of the block.

   Note: For speedy piecing, try chain piecing these blocks as described at right.

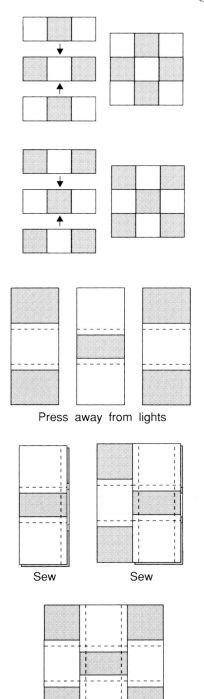

Press away from lights

Sew   Sew

Completed block
(wrong side)

Chain Piecing

Chain piecing is a shortcut to take when many patches are to be sewn. This technique is best suited to simple blocks and repetitious steps. It helps to organize the pairs and stack them in order before starting to sew.

1. Place the first pair of patches (or strip-pieced segments as in this block), right sides together, under the presser foot. (Pinning is optional.)

2. Stitch the seam; do not lift the presser foot or cut threads at the end of the patch. Just stop sewing and place the next pair of patches under the presser foot about ¼" in front of the needle. Stitch "in the air" for several stitches to create a chain that locks the thread. The feed dog will grip the next pair of patches and pull them under the needle. When the "chains" are complete, snip them apart. Add the next patch (or segment) in the same manner.

Eight-Pointed Star Blocks

For this block, you will need to make templates, using the patterns on page 17 and following the template-making directions on page 16. Many of the other patchwork designs that you will encounter in your quiltmaking career require templates as well.

The template patterns in this book are marked with the name of the block, the finished size of the block in which it is used, and the number of pieces to cut to make one block. It's a good idea to mark this information on the template you make for possible re-use later.

Directions

Make one Eight-Pointed Star Block.

1. Make Templates A, B, and C and cut the required number of each template from the fabrics you've chosen, following the template-making directions on page 16.

2. Thread a size 7 or 8 quilting needle with an 18"-long strand of cotton sewing thread and knot at one end.

3. Place 2 diamond patches (Template A) with right sides together. Insert a pin into the corner dot of the top patch and push it through to the matching corner on the bottom patch. Repeat with the dots at the other end of the seam. Then, secure the pins so they hold the patches in place for sewing. New quilters also find it helpful to place a pin in the center of the seam for added control while sewing.

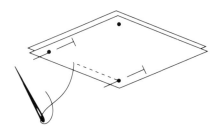

4. Insert the needle exactly in the corner dot at the outside point of the star and sew

the patches together with a tiny running stitch ¼" from the raw edges. Pack about 4 or 5 stitches on the needle at a time and backstitch every inch or so to secure the seam. Remove pins as you stitch. Sew to the seam-intersection dot at the opposite end of the seam and backstitch to secure the stitching. Do not sew past the seam intersection!

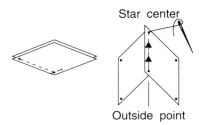

Star center

Outside point

5. Leaving the threaded needle in place at the center point, pin the next diamond in place at the center and outer corner dots to create a unit of 3 diamonds. Stitch from the center dot to the corner dot at the outside point of the third diamond. Secure with several stitches in place and cut the thread. Create another unit of 3 diamonds in the same way.

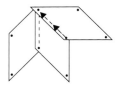

6. Add the fourth diamond to the units of 3, to create each half of the star. Sew from the center out, making sure that the center point where the 4 points meet is connected securely.

Note: When piecing stars, sew from the outside corner "dot" toward the center. At the halfway point on the seam, sew the remaining half of the seam one needle's width inside the seam line (into the seam allowance). This helps the blocks lie flat. Otherwise they may tend to "pooch up."

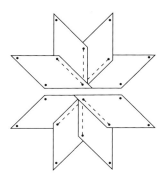

7. Join the 2 units of 4 diamonds each, creating a complete star. As you stitch, keep the seam allowances of each diamond out of the way so that you do not stitch them down in the center. Pinning right at the center where the seams converge helps.

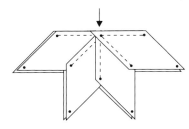

8. Press the seams in the same direction, pinwheel-fashion, around the center. A small star will form in the center of the block.

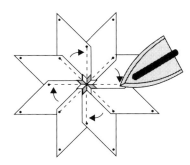

9. To set in the corners (Template B) and triangles (Template C), pin one side to the diamond, matching dots at seam intersections. Sew from the outer edge to the inside corner. *Do not sew even one stitch past the corner dot into the seam allowance,* or the corner will not lie flat. Backstitch at the corner, but do not cut the threads.

Pin the remaining side of the square or triangle and continue sewing toward the dot at the outer edge. Repeat with remaining inset pieces until the block is complete.

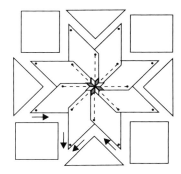

10. Pinwheel-press the corner seams so they lie flat. Follow the previous star pressing as a guide for the correct direction to press.

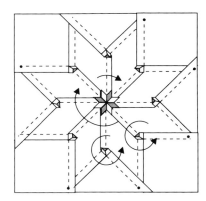

Notice how beginning and ending the seams at the seam intersections during hand piecing allows you more pressing options than the previous speedy machine-piecing methods on the Ninepatch blocks. It is not necessarily better, just a different option. The more complicated the block (for example, pieced stars with diamonds or lots of pieces on the bias), the more accurate it is for a novice quilter to hand piece. But a simple block, with all pieces cut square and on the straight of grain, such as the Ninepatch, lends itself well to machine piecing.

Making and Using Templates

Supplies

paper	*sharp pencil*
paper scissors	*template plastic*
darning needle	*fabric spray glue*
or rubber cement	

Directions

1. Trace template patterns onto paper, marking the stitching lines as well as the cutting lines. Mark the grain-line arrow.

2. Cut template from paper, leaving an extra ¼" of paper outside the cutting line all around the shape.

3. Apply fabric spray glue or rubber cement to the back of each paper pattern and position on the template plastic. Smooth paper in place so it is wrinkle-free.

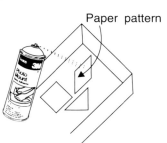

Paper pattern

4. Cut the template(s) from the plastic on the drawn lines. Do not cut outside the line or the template will be too large. If you cut inside the line, it will be too small.

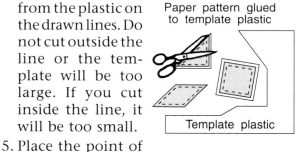

Paper pattern glued to template plastic

Template plastic

5. Place the point of a large darning needle into a candle flame until it is hot. (Stick the other end of the needle in a cork so your fingers don't get burned while heating the needle.) Use the point of the hot needle to pierce the template at the seam-line intersections. Wiggle the needle to make the hole about ¹⁄₁₆" around so you can mark through the hole with a marking pen.

6. To use the templates, place face down on the wrong side of the fabric, being careful to position the template with the grain-line arrow on the lengthwise or crosswise grain of the fabric. That way, the patches will be cut so the outer edges of the completed block will be on the straight grain and will not stretch out of shape during handling. Trace around the template onto the fabric with a soft, washable pencil or silver pencil.

Wrong side of fabric

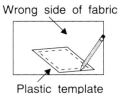

Plastic template

7. Cut *on* the marked cutting line, *not inside or outside the line.* Cut carefully! What you cut is what you piece!

Note: The rotary cutter is perfect for cutting several layers at one time. Or, if your scissors are sharp, you may stack up to 4 layers of fabric. Pin the fabric layers together with flat-headed pins so the layers don't shift while cutting. For rotary cutting, use a short acrylic ruler as a guide for the cutter.

Use flat-headed pins

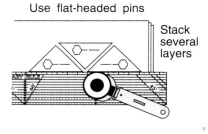

Stack several layers

8. Mark seam-allowance intersections on each block through the holes you made in the templates.

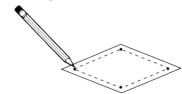

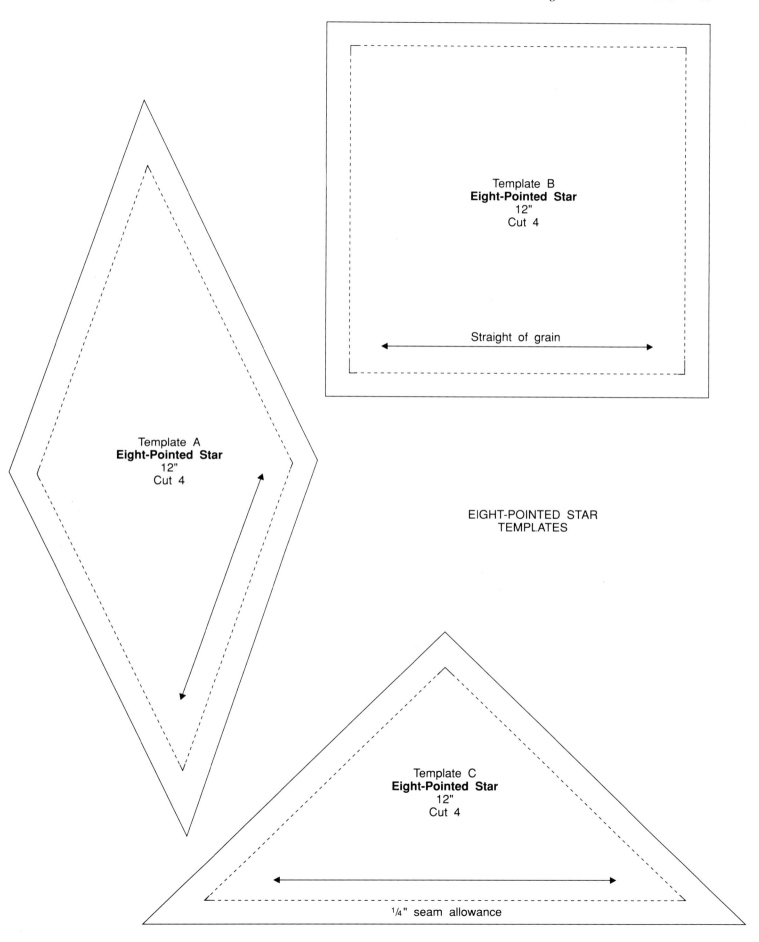

Template B
Eight-Pointed Star
12"
Cut 4

Straight of grain

Template A
Eight-Pointed Star
12"
Cut 4

EIGHT-POINTED STAR
TEMPLATES

Template C
Eight-Pointed Star
12"
Cut 4

¹/4" seam allowance

Pieced Blocks with Half-Square Triangles

The trick to sewing triangles together is not to stretch the longer bias edge and to allow enough seam allowance for piecing the diagonal seam. The speedy method shown below eliminates both concerns.

Following the directions, make 32 half-square triangle blocks, 4½" x 4½". Then use these blocks to make 2 to 4 pieced blocks based on a Ninepatch grid for the Kansas Sampler quilt. Suggested block designs appear on page 20.

Directions

Make two to four Pieced Blocks with Half-Square Triangles.

1. Cut a 20" square of a light-colored fabric and a 20" square of a dark-colored fabric.
2. Place the squares right sides together with the lightest color on top.
3. Determine the marking size for the triangles by adding ⅞" to the desired finished half-square triangle block. In this block, the finished block must be 4" to create Ninepatch designs. Therefore, the marking size is 4⅞". For ease in measuring and marking, place a piece of masking tape on your ruler along the 4⅞" mark.
4. Mark a right angle on the light-colored fabric; then mark a grid of 4⅞" squares as shown.

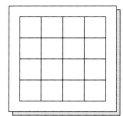

Wrong side

Mark a 4⅞" grid on the top of fabric

5. Next, mark diagonally across the corners of the grid, creating the triangles. Do not trim away the excess fabric around the outer edge of the marked squares.

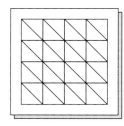

6. Mark sewing lines, ¼" away from the diagonal lines on both sides of the line.

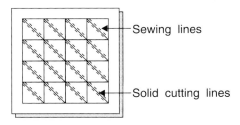

Sewing lines

Solid cutting lines

7. Pin the fabric layers together so they don't shift during sewing.

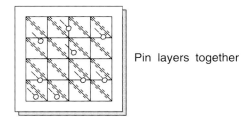

Pin layers together

Shorten the stitch length on the machine to 20 stitches per inch. Sew on the sewing lines on each side of the diagonal lines. It's not necessary to cut the thread at the end of each row of stitching. Instead, lift the presser foot, pull some slack in the threads, and move over to the next marked stitching line. Remove pins if they interfere with your sewing progress.

8. When the sewing is complete, trim away the excess fabric around the outer edges of the grid and cut the blocks apart on the solid lines.

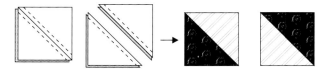

You should have 32 half-square triangle blocks that each measure 4½" square. Do not press yet.

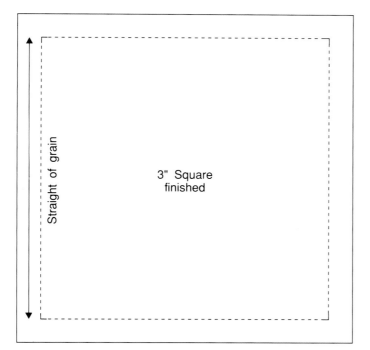

HALF-SQUARE
TRIANGLE BLOCK
TEMPLATES

Use the 3" square to make 16-patch, half-square designs.

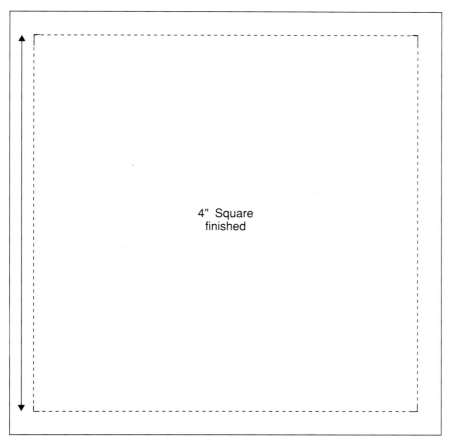

Use the 4" square to make Ninepatch half-square designs.

Blocks Based on a Ninepatch Grid

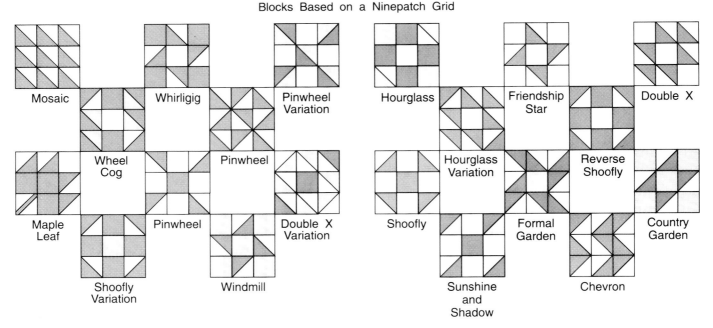

Mosaic | Whirligig | Pinwheel Variation

Wheel Cog | Pinwheel

Maple Leaf | Pinwheel | Double X Variation

Shoofly Variation | Windmill

Hourglass | Friendship Star | Double X

Hourglass Variation | Reverse Shoofly

Shoofly | Formal Garden | Country Garden

Sunshine and Shadow | Chevron

9. Use the half-square triangle blocks with 4½" squares cut from solid-colored fabric to make 2 to 4 blocks based on a Nine-patch grid. Choose from those shown above.

   Note: To cut 4½" squares, use the 4½"-square template on page 19. Or, rotary cut 4½"-wide strips and crosscut the strips into 4½" squares.

Each block illustrated above requires its own pressing solution, and you will need to decide whether to machine or hand piece. In general, it's best to press seams toward the darker fabrics so the seams don't shadow through to the right side of the finished block.

For machine-pieced blocks, press seams that must match precisely in opposing directions. For hand-pieced blocks, press pinwheel fashion as described for the hand-pieced Eight-Pointed Star on page 15.

Now make 32 half-square triangle blocks, 3½" x 3½", to use in blocks based on a 16-patch grid. There are lots of seam allowances in 16-patch blocks, so use a scant ¼"-wide seam allowance during the sewing to make sure the assembled block will not be less than 12½" square (12" finished).

1. Cut 1 light-colored and 1 dark-colored 18" square of fabric.
2. Layer fabrics right sides together and mark the grid lines at 3⅞". Mark the diagonal cutting lines and the stitching lines as shown for the 4⅞" grid on page 18. Stitch and cut apart as directed for the 4⅞" grid.
3. Using the template on page 19, make a 3½"-square template. Use to cut assorted 3½" fabric squares to mix with the half-square triangle blocks to make any of the designs shown on page 21. Or, rotary cut 3½"-wide strips and crosscut the strips into 3½" squares. Make 2 to 4 blocks of your choice.

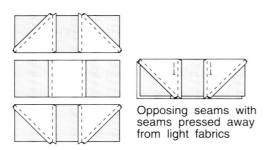

Opposing seams with seams pressed away from light fabrics

Using Grid Sheets

At Osage County Quilt Factory, our favorite method for sewing half-square triangle blocks is to use paper grid sheets like those stapled in the center of this book. This accurate and quick method takes the place of marking the stitching and cutting grid described on page 18.

1. Cut the grid sheet into manageable sections of 4- or 6-block units, depending on how many blocks you need of a color combination.
2. Layer the light and dark fabrics with right sides together. Pin the grid sheet to the fabrics using flat-headed pins.

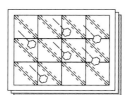

Grid sheet

Two fabrics right sides together

3. Shorten machine stitch to 20 stitches per inch.
4. Stitch on the dotted lines and cut on the solid lines, separating each block.

 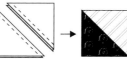

5. Tear away the paper, tearing from the center out. This helps keep the stitches from coming unsewn while removing the paper.
6. Press seams toward dark fabrics and use blocks to create larger blocks based on Ninepatch or 16-patch grids as shown.

Blocks Based on a 16-Patch Grid

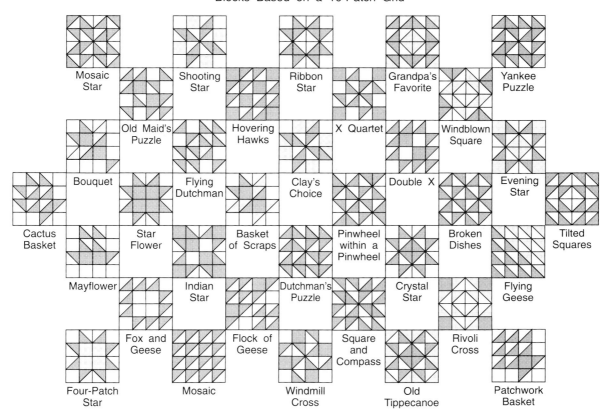

Mosaic Star · Shooting Star · Ribbon Star · Grandpa's Favorite · Yankee Puzzle

Old Maid's Puzzle · Hovering Hawks · X Quartet · Windblown Square

Bouquet · Flying Dutchman · Clay's Choice · Double X · Evening Star

Cactus Basket · Star Flower · Basket of Scraps · Pinwheel within a Pinwheel · Broken Dishes · Tilted Squares

Mayflower · Indian Star · Dutchman's Puzzle · Crystal Star · Flying Geese

Fox and Geese · Flock of Geese · Square and Compass · Rivoli Cross

Four-Patch Star · Mosaic · Windmill Cross · Old Tippecanoe · Patchwork Basket

Log Cabin Blocks

The Log Cabin is a favorite traditional block that is easy to piece by hand or machine. The center of the Log Cabin is most often cut from an accent ("popper") color. One-half of the block surrounding the center square is cut from 3 different dark-colored fabrics and the remaining half from 3 different light-colored fabrics, so you will need 7 different fabrics for a Log Cabin block.

Directions

Make four Log Cabin blocks.

1. From your fabrics, select an accent or "popper" color for the center square and 3 lights and 3 darks for the "logs."
2. Cut light and dark strips and a center square from the appropriate fabrics and paste up a sample block, using a glue stick to hold them in position on the diagram (or a tracing of it).

3. From the accent color, cut a 3½" x 14" strip for the centers, being sure not to include any of the selvage in the strip. From each of 3 different light fabrics and from each of 3 different dark fabrics, cut 2 strips, each 2" x 44". You should have a total of 12 strips, 6 light and 6 dark.

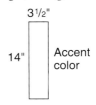

4. Arrange the strips to the side of your sewing area in the order shown. This is the order of sewing; except for the center fabric, each fabric will be used twice in each block you make.

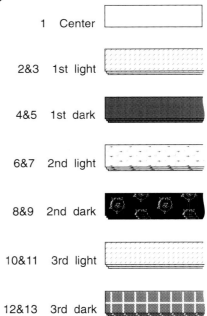

5. With right sides together, stitch the center strip to the first light strip ¼" from one long edge. Do not include any selvage in the seam.

Note: Since Log Cabin blocks have lots of seams, it helps to sew *scant*

¼"-*wide seams* on these blocks (closer to ³⁄₁₆"). This prevents the block from being less than the required 12½" when assembled.

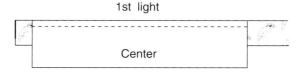

Press the seams toward the light strip, away from the center.

Note: All pressing in Log Cabin blocks is away from the center.

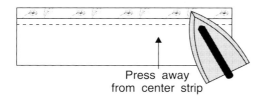

Press away from center strip

6. Crosscut the strip pair into 3½"-wide segments. You should have 4, one for each block you are making.

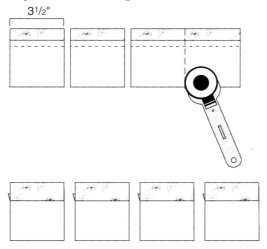

3½"

7. Place the center block units right side down and to the left of the sewing machine. Position so the light strip is at the top and the center square is toward you. Place another first light strip right side up on the sewing machine. Place one of the center block units face down on top of the light strip, positioning it ¼" below the selvage. Sew the center block unit to the light strip, taking care not to twist the seam you must stitch across. Before reaching the end of the block, butt another block along the strip right next to the

first. Continue sewing, repeating for all 4 blocks. Cut the blocks apart, using the edge of the center block as the cutting guide. Press seams away from the centers.

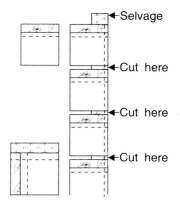

Selvage
Cut here
Cut here
Cut here

Note: If you prefer, you may press the blocks, pressing the seams away from the center while they are still in a "chain." Then, fold the strip back into stitching position and cut the blocks apart, using the edge of the center blocks as the guide for cutting.

8. Place the blocks face down on the table with the most recently added light strip at the top.

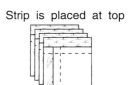

Strip is placed at top

Place the first dark 2"-wide strip right side up on the sewing machine and place a block face down on top, ¼" below the selvage. Sew the blocks to the strip as before, taking care not to twist the pressed seams in the opposite direction during the sewing. Cut blocks apart and press as before.

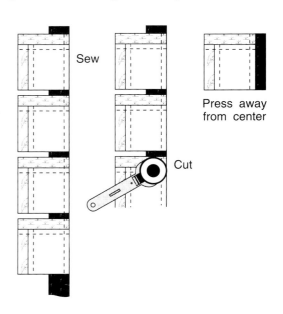

Sew

Cut

Press away from center

Add another first dark strip to the block in the same manner.

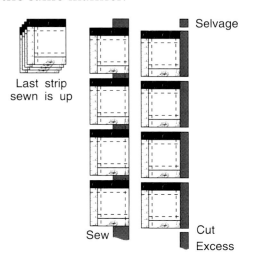

Last strip sewn is up

Selvage

Sew

Cut

Excess

9. Add 2 second light strips to the block in the same manner.

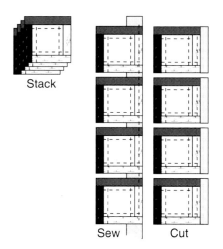

Stack

Sew

Cut

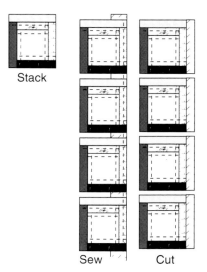

Stack

Sew

Cut

10. Add 2 second dark strips to the block.

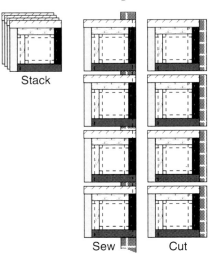

Stack

Sew

Cut

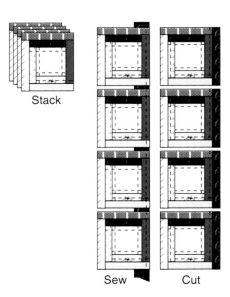

Stack

Sew

Cut

11. Add 2 third light strips to the block.

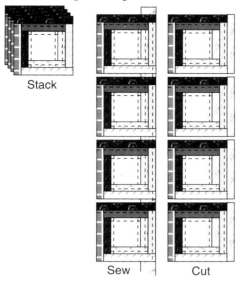

Stack

Sew · Cut

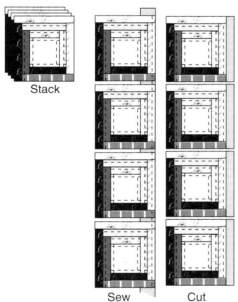

Stack

Sew Cut

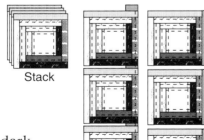

Stack

12. Add 2 third dark strips to the block.

Sew Cut

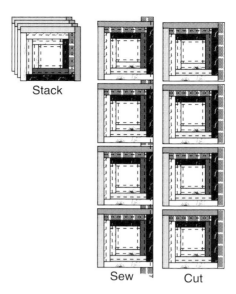

Stack

Sew Cut

When you have finished your Log Cabin blocks, you should have some 2"-wide strips left over. Use these for the string blocks that follow. Log Cabin blocks can be arranged in the same manner as half-square triangle blocks, with dark and light sides creating the designs. You can use the four blocks you've made to create a small center medallion for your sampler quilt or to create direction in your quilt top. You may wish to make more Log Cabin blocks as your quilt design evolves.

Two rules apply to the sewing process for Log Cabin blocks:

1. Always press the seams toward the "logs," away from the center square.
2. After adding each log, stack the blocks face down, with the most recently added "log" at the top of the stack.

String Blocks

String blocks are sewn on paper to stabilize the bias edges that result. You can use typing paper or anything in a similar weight. This block is used creatively in the sampler quilts shown in this book. When created as a half-light, half-dark block, a String block adds direction and design to the quilt. String blocks use up a lot of scraps, too—a nice bonus! Cut 2"-wide strips from a variety of your fabrics.

Directions

Make two to four String blocks.

1. Cut a 12½" square of typing paper. Fold the paper on the diagonal from corner to corner.

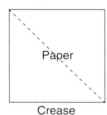

2. Fold the first 2"-wide strip of fabric (left over from the Log Cabin blocks) in half lengthwise and press. Place this strip exactly in the center of the paper, lining up the marked diagonal fold line on the paper with the fold in the fabric. Pin or use a glue stick to glue the strip to the paper, right side up.

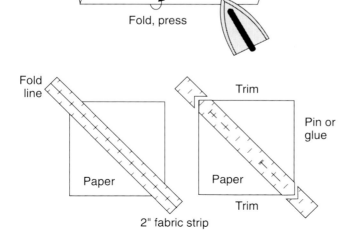

3. Place the next 2"-wide fabric strip face down on the first strip and sew ¼" away from one long edge.

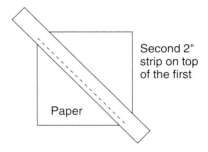

4. Flip the sewn strip back and press. Trim the fabric strip, using the paper edge as your guide.

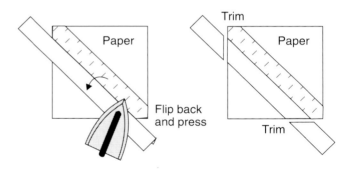

5. Repeat the process on the other side of the center strip. Continue the process until the entire square of paper is covered with strips. Do not remove the paper backing until after the blocks are set together with your other blocks and lattice strips (page 35).

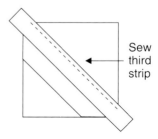

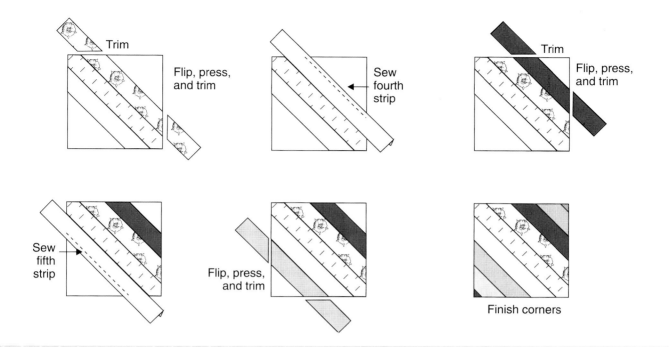

Trim

Flip, press, and trim

Sew fourth strip

Trim

Flip, press, and trim

Sew fifth strip

Flip, press, and trim

Finish corners

Design Options:

You may want to experiment with additional String blocks, making them larger and then cutting them into smaller squares to create new block designs like those shown below. Be sure to allow for ¼"-wide seams, starting with the larger paper size indicated with each block design.

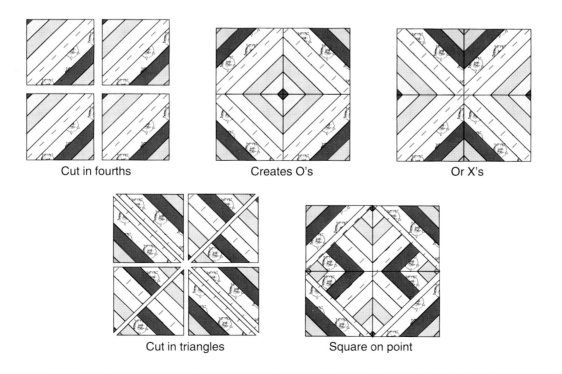

Cut in fourths

Creates O's

Or X's

Cut in triangles

Square on point

String Quilt Design Ideas

You can design an entire quilt top, using only String blocks arranged into "X" and "O" formations as shown in the diagrams, below.

It is important to remember to piece the entire quilt top with the paper attached to the blocks so the bias edges don't stretch. Remove the paper before quilting.

You can also use String blocks to create wonderful zigzag borders.

Dresden Plate

The Dresden Plate is a popular traditional block that requires hand appliqué. You will learn a simple technique for perfect appliquéd circles. Two versions of the Dresden Plate are given here. The first has curved sections and the second has pointed ones. You will learn the appropriate construction techniques for each one.

Cut the Dresden Plate sections from any of your light and dark fabrics. Cut the center from the accent or "popper" fabric and use your lightest, least-busy print for the background of the block. Make one or two Dresden Plate blocks in your choice of design.

Directions for Curved Dresden Plate
Make one or two Dresden Plate blocks.
1. Make Templates A and C, using those found on page 31 and following the template-making directions on page 16.
2. Make a cardboard template for the inner circle of Template C. I use cereal-box cardboard for this.
3. For each block, cut 16 plate sections (Template A) and 1 center (Template C) from the chosen fabrics, using your plastic templates to mark them onto your fabrics.
4. Use a small running stitch (or 6 stitches per inch on the sewing machine) to stitch ⅛" from the outer edge of the center circle (Template C). Place the cardboard circle in the center of the fabric circle on the wrong side. Pull up the stitches tightly to gather the edge of the fabric snugly around the cardboard circle. Press firmly.

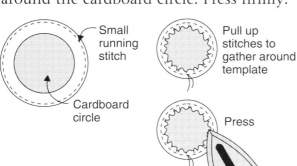

Small running stitch

Cardboard circle

Pull up stitches to gather around template

Press

Now pop the cardboard out of the fabric circle, leaving a perfectly shaped and pressed circle ready for appliqué.
5. Sew the plate sections together in pairs, sewing scant ¼"-wide seams. Begin stitching at the seam intersection at the outer edge of the section and stitch to the center. Sew the pairs together to complete the Dresden Plate. Pinwheel-press the seams in the same direction until the Dresden Plate lies flat.

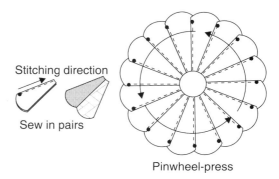

Stitching direction

Sew in pairs

Pinwheel-press

6. Make a cardboard template of the outside curve of the plate section (shaded area of Template B).

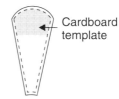

Cardboard template

7. Sew a row of short running stitches ⅛" from the raw edge of the curve on each fan section and pull up the stitches tightly to gather the edges over the cardboard template as shown. Press; remove cardboard template.

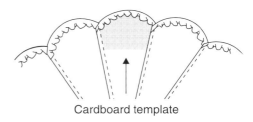

Cardboard template

8. Cut a 12½" square of the lightest fabric for the background block. Position completed plate in the center of the block and with a glue stick, glue in place. Position and glue center circle over the raw edges in the center of the Dresden Plate.

9. Thread an appliqué needle (size 11 or 12 Sharp) with fine (machine embroidery) thread in a color matching the fabric circle. Knot one end and start stitching with the knot on the back side of the project. Come up through the edge of the circle and go right back down through to the background with a tiny, tiny stitch that doesn't show when pulled tight. Come up again in the circle ⅟₃₂"–⅟₁₆" ahead of the last stitch and take another stitch. Continue around the circle, taking care not to pleat or distort the circle. Appliqué outer edges of the plate in the same way.

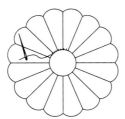

Directions for Pointed Dresden Plate

If you prefer the more angular Dresden Plate, make one or two of these blocks instead of the Curved Dresden Plate blocks.

1. Make plastic templates for Templates B and C, using those found on page 31 and following the template-making directions on page 16.
2. Make a cardboard template for the inner circle of Template C as shown on page 29.
3. Cut plate sections from chosen fabrics, using your plastic templates to trace them onto your fabrics.
4. Prepare the center circle as shown in step 4 for Curved Dresden Plate.
5. Fold each plate section in half, right sides together, and stitch across the top, ¼" from the edge as shown.

Sew→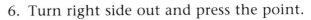

6. Turn right side out and press the point.

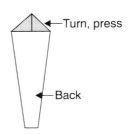

7. Sew the plate sections together in pairs, sewing a scant ¼"-wide seam. Stitch from the outer point to the inner circle. Sew the pairs together to complete the Dresden Plate and pinwheel-press as shown in step 5 for Curved Dresden Plate.

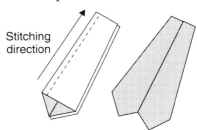

Stitching direction

8. Cut a 12½" square of the lightest fabric for the background block. Center and pin plate in place on the background square to keep it from shifting. Pin or glue circle in place over the raw edges in the center of the block. Appliqué the center circle as shown in step 9 for the Curved Dresden Plate.

9. To appliqué outer edges of plate, begin stitching at the inner point of one section and stitch to the outer point. Secure the point with several tiny stitches in place. Continue stitching to next inner point and secure. Repeat around entire plate.

Several tiny stitches   Start here

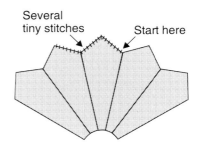

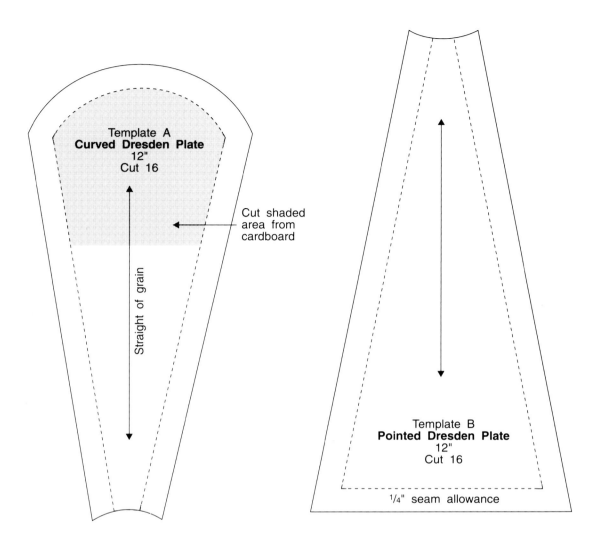

Template A
Curved Dresden Plate
12"
Cut 16

Cut shaded area from cardboard

Straight of grain

Template B
Pointed Dresden Plate
12"
Cut 16

¼" seam allowance

DRESDEN PLATE
TEMPLATES

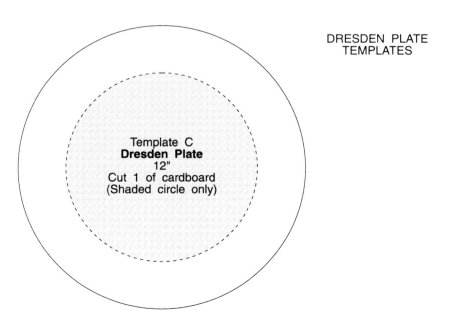

Template C
Dresden Plate
12"
Cut 1 of cardboard
(Shaded circle only)

Grandmother's Fan

While making these Grandmother's Fan blocks, you will learn to do curved piecing. Instead of appliquéing the quarter-circle in the corner of the block, you will stitch it to the inner curve of the pieced fan blades instead. Then, you will appliqué the completed fan to a background block. Make at least 4 of these blocks.

From your fabric selection, choose a light background color for the block, a color for the center of the fan, and a variety of fabrics in light and dark colors for the fan blades.

Directions

Make four Grandmother's Fan Blocks.

1. Make plastic templates of Templates A and B on page 33, following the template-making directions on page 16.

2. For each block, cut one 12½" square of background fabric. Cut 8 fan blades (Template A) and 1 quarter-circle (Template B).

3. Fold each fan blade in half, right sides together, and stitch across the top, ¼" from the raw edge as shown.

Sew

4. Turn blades right side out and press the points.

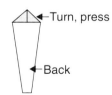
Turn, press

Back

Assemble the fan and press all seams in one direction as shown in step 5 for the Curved Dresden Plate on page 29.

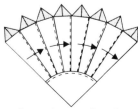
Press in one direction

5. Fold the quarter-circle in half and then in half again. Crease the folds firmly to mark the half- and quarter-points at the outer curved edges.

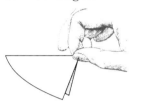
Finger press

Crease lines

6. Pin the outer curved edge of the quarter-circle to the inner curve of the fan, matching the center crease to the center seam and the quarter-point creases to the second and sixth seams.

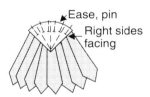
Ease, pin
Right sides facing

7. Stitch the quarter-circle to the fan, easing into position as you sew. Piece by hand or machine. Press the seam toward the fan.

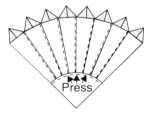
Press

8. Position the completed fan on the background block with the raw edges of the quarter-circle even with the outer edges of the block. Pin or glue in place. Appliqué to the background as shown in step 9 for the Pointed Dresden Plate on page 30.

9. Trim away the excess background fabric behind the fan, leaving a ¼-wide seam allowance.

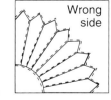
Wrong side

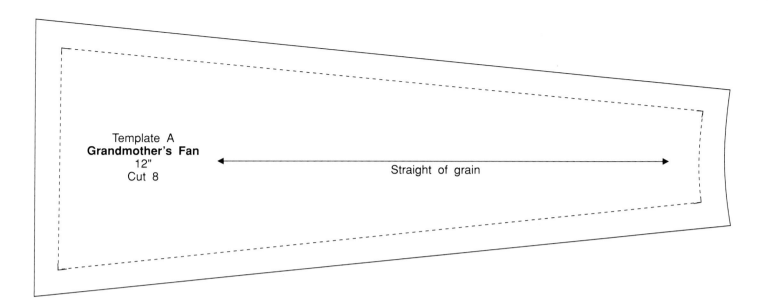

Template A
Grandmother's Fan
12"
Cut 8

Straight of grain

GRANDMOTHER'S FAN
TEMPLATES

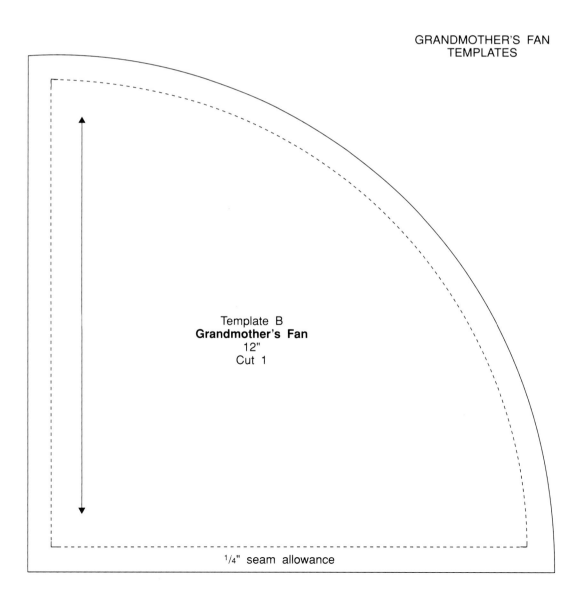

Template B
Grandmother's Fan
12"
Cut 1

1/4" seam allowance

Crazy Quilt Blocks

Here's your chance to use up your scraps in colorful, random-pieced Crazy Quilt blocks. These blocks are pieced on a paper foundation square like the String blocks on page 26.

Directions
Make two to four Crazy Quilt blocks.
1. For each block, cut a 12½" square of paper.
2. Place a scrap of fabric face up in the center of the paper. Place another scrap face down on top so the raw edges match. Stitch ¼" from the matched edge. Flip the scrap back and press. Trim. Repeat with another scrap. Keep the edges of each piece straight rather than curved for easier, quicker sewing. Be careful not to work yourself into an outside corner where a piece will have to be appliquéd.

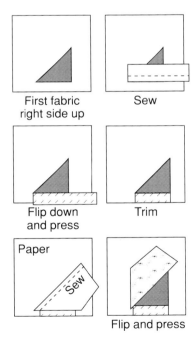

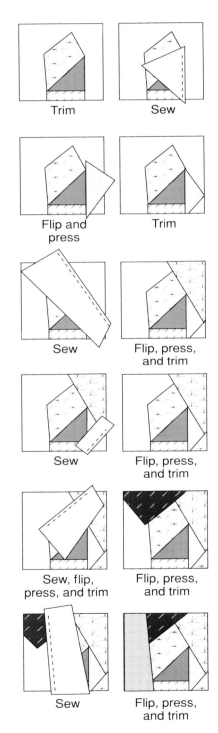

3. Continue piecing, pressing, and trimming until the paper is covered with colorful scraps. (Trim the scraps even with the edges of the paper.) To prevent the bias edges from stretching, *do not tear away the paper until the block is set into the quilt top.*

Let's Make a Quilt!

Now that you have completed your sampler blocks, you're ready to make them into a quilt top. You will need to add lattice strips between the blocks, then add batting and backing and quilt the layers together. The final step is binding the edges to finish your masterpiece.

Planning the Quilt Top Layout

First, make sure all your sampler blocks are 12½" square. If there is a size variation of more than ⅛", correct all blocks by trimming them to the size of the smallest block. Be sure to leave the foundation paper on the String and Crazy Quilt blocks until you've sewn the blocks and lattice strips together to complete the quilt top.

Next, determine how large your quilt will be. You can simply arrange your sampler blocks in a pleasing pattern, add lattice strips, and sew them together to create a wall hanging or lap quilt, or you can plan to use them in a quilt to fit a specific bed.

If you are planning the quilt for a bed, measure the bed as shown. Decide whether you want the quilt to fall to the floor (bedspread length) or just to the bottom edge of the mattress (comforter size). Will you use pillow shams or will the quilt need to cover and tuck under pillows? Allow an extra 9" to 10" in length for a pillow tuck beyond the total length of the mattress plus the drop at the foot of the bed.

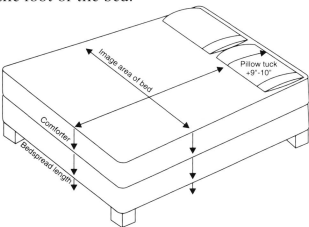

The chart below gives some general guidelines for standard quilt measurements.

Bed Size	Quilt Size	
	Comforter	Bedspread
Twin (39" x 75")	63" x 87"	80" x 106"
Double (54" x 75")	78" x 87"	95" x 106"
Queen (60" x 80")	84" x 92"	101" x 112"
King (76" x 80")	100"x 92"	117" x 112"

Draw the desired outer dimensions of the quilt to scale on graph paper so you can arrange blocks and figure the widths for the lattice strips and borders. Lattice strips are narrow bands of fabric used to join the blocks, yet allow them to stand alone within the quilt top.

In planning block placement, it's nice to arrange the blocks and lattices so the edges of the lattice or blocks end at the edge of the image area of the bed. To aid you in doing this, mark the image area of the bed on the quilt plan, then arrange blocks inside the area, allowing room for the lattice strips.

Your quilt can have plain lattices or lattices with corner blocks.

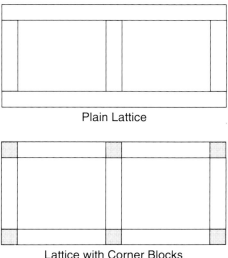

Plain Lattice

Lattice with Corner Blocks

Plain Lattices

1. Cut the lattice strips to the desired width. The lattice width is partly determined by the finished quilt size. It is also determined by the proportion that looks right with the blocks. A general rule of proportion is to use a measurement that matches a finished measurement of one of the components in a quilt block.

   For example, you made some blocks using 3" (finished) half-square triangle units and some using 4" (finished) half-square triangle units. Therefore, a 3"- or 4"-wide (finished) lattice would be a good width to use for the lattice strips. If the lattice is a stripe, then let the stripe determine the lattice width. *Avoid making the lattices wider than 5".*

   As you plan your quilt-top arrangement, you might find it necessary to make additional blocks or add borders to enlarge the quilt top.

2. Following your graph-paper plan, arrange the quilt blocks on the floor, a large table, or a bed.

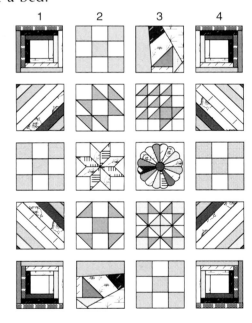

   Pick up the first row of blocks in order and chain-sew the left-hand edge of each to a lattice strip (just like assembling speedy Log Cabin blocks, page 22). Cut apart.

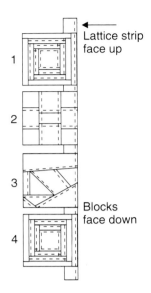

Lattice strip face up

Blocks face down

Press the seams away from the block. Put the blocks back into position on your work area. Pick up the next row of quilt blocks and stitch them to the lattice strips as before. Repeat until all the blocks have a lattice strip on one side. Then add a lattice strip to the blocks at the remaining right-hand edge of the block to the far right of the row.

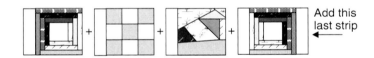

Add this last strip

3. Join the quilt blocks into rows across the width of the quilt.

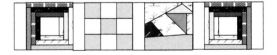

4. Pin the first row of blocks to a lattice the width of the quilt top and sew. Be very careful not to stretch the lattice or the blocks while sewing. Continue adding long lattice strips between the rows. Add a lattice strip to both sides of the top and bottom rows.

5. To help line up the blocks and lattices, mark placement lines as shown, using a washable marking pen or chalk pencil. Starting from the top of the quilt and

working down, pin and sew the top 2 rows together. Add the third row to them. Continue until the quilt top is complete. Press all seams toward the lattice strips.

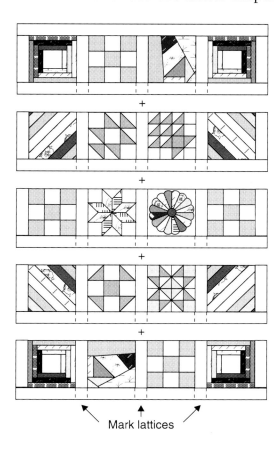

Mark lattices

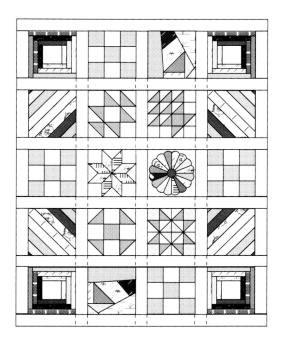

Lattices with Corner Blocks

1. Cut and add short lattice strips between the blocks in each row as described for plain lattices. Join blocks with lattice into rows.

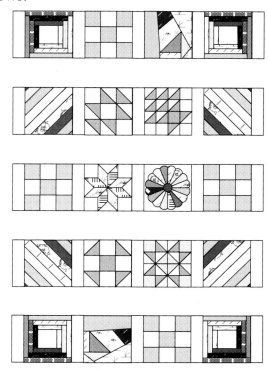

Join rows across

2. Cut the lattice strips the length of the quilt blocks including ½" for seam allowances (12½", in this case), cutting across the width or along the length of the fabric as desired. If the fabric design is directional (a stripe, for example), be sure to decide how you want it to appear in the quilt before cutting the strips.

Cut strips for the corner blocks to match the cut width of the lattice strips.

With right sides together, stitch the corner-block strips to the lattice strips, using a ¼"-wide seam allowance.

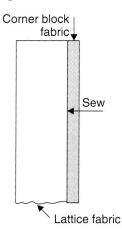

Corner block fabric

Sew

Lattice fabric

3. Cut the corner block/lattice units the width of the lattice. For example, if the finished lattice is to be 3", cut the corner/lattice 3½". Assemble the lattice/corner block units into pieced-lattice strip lengths the width of the quilt.

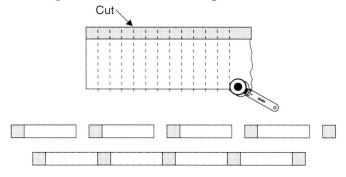

Press with seams in opposing directions to the lattice seams in the row to which the strip will be joined, making the seams easier to match. Join the rows of blocks with lattice strips as described for Plain Lattices in step 5, page 36.

Add lattice with
corner blocks

Completed Top
(borders optional)

Borders

Most of the quilts in this book were designed with borders as the finishing design element. Some have multiple borders, and several contain pieced elements for added visual interest. Directions for the pieced borders are given with the individual quilts.

Plan the borders for your quilt on graph paper as you arrange the other elements of your quilt—blocks and lattice strips. Borders may be straight cut or mitered. Straight-cut borders are often easier for beginning quiltmakers.

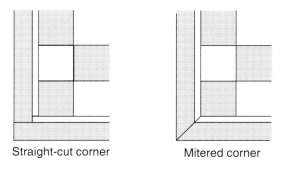

Straight-cut corner   Mitered corner

When borders are included in the quilt instructions, directions for cutting the required number of strips are given, but specific lengths for each border strip are not. Instead, you must measure the finished quilt top, then cut the border strips to the correct length for each border. This allows for individual quilt-makers' variations in cutting and piecing, which can cause a quilt to finish to a different size than the finished dimensions given for the quilt. It also ensures that the finished quilt will be "true" or "square" rather than distorted in shape.

Straight-Cut Borders

1. Measure the length of the quilt at the center and cut 2 border strips to that measurement.

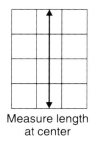

Measure length
at center

2. Fold quilt in half crosswise and mark centers of each side with pins. Repeat with the 2 border strips.
3. Pin borders to sides, matching centers and ends. Stitch the side borders to the quilt, easing or stretching to fit as needed. Press seams toward borders.

    Note: One or both outside edges of the quilt may not be the same measurement as the center of the quilt. Cutting both borders exactly the same length as the center, then easing or stretching to fit as needed makes the quilt come out square.

4. Measure the width of the quilt top, plus side borders, and cut 2 border strips to that length. Attach borders to top and bottom as described for side borders.

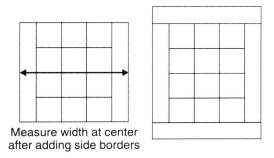

Measure width at center
after adding side borders

Mitered Borders

1. Estimate the finished outside dimensions of your quilt, including the border(s). Refer to your quilt plan on graph paper.
2. Cut side borders to the length of the *outside dimension, plus no less than ½" for seam allowances.* Just to be safe, many quilters prefer to add an extra 2" to 3" to the length of each border strip.

    Note: If your quilt has multiple borders, piece the borders together for each side of the quilt and then attach to the quilt edges as strip-pieced units.

3. Fold quilt and border strips in half and mark the centers of each with pins.
4. Measure the length and width of the quilt top at the centers. Note measurements.
5. On the side border strips, place pins to mark the length of the quilt. Repeat with the top and bottom border strips.

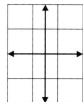

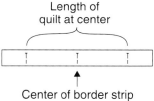

Length of
quilt at center

Center of border strip

6. Pin side borders to quilt, matching centers and having remaining pins in border at top and bottom edges of quilt. Stitch to quilt, using a ¼"-wide seam allowance and beginning and ending stitching ¼" in from the corners. Repeat with top and bottom borders.

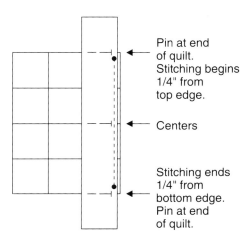

Pin at end of quilt. Stitching begins 1/4" from top edge.

Centers

Stitching ends 1/4" from bottom edge. Pin at end of quilt.

7. Place one corner of quilt on ironing board, right side up, and pin in place. Fold under one border strip at a 45° angle. Pin. Use a clear acrylic ruler with a 45° angle to check the corner, making sure it's square and the angle is true. Press.

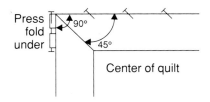

8. Slipstitch the folded edge in place.

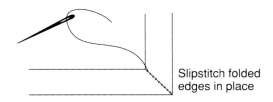

Slipstitch folded edges in place

If you prefer to machine stitch the mitered corner, center a strip of 1"-wide masking tape over the mitered fold, removing pins as you go. Remove quilt from ironing board.

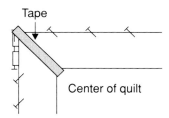

On inside, fold the quilt as shown, lining up the edges of the border. Use a ruler and pencil to draw a stitching line on the border. Stitch. Remove tape. Trim away excess border, leaving a ¼"-wide seam allowance. Press seam open.

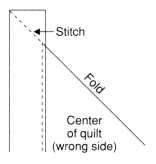

9. Repeat with remaining corners.

Batting Hints and Helps

Good-quality batting will not crush. It has resiliency and memory so that the quilt will stay puffy over the years. Many types of quilt batting are available and each has its own merits. Ask for assistance in selecting batting at your favorite quilt shop. I recommend avoiding batting that is bonded on only one surface as it is likely to shift inside the quilt, causing twists and wrinkles during quilting. It will also have a tendency to migrate to the outside, causing pilling (little polyester balls on the surface of the quilt). Unbonded batting is difficult to separate into layers, resulting in uneven thickness.

A low-loft batting is easier to quilt and does not distort the edges of the quilt. The high-loft battings are especially suited for tied comforters. (See page 45.)

Needlepunched wool and cotton batting with a low loft are excellent. They are natural fibers that breathe. The wool battings are especially nice because the lanolin helps lubricate the needle during quilting so it glides more easily through the layers.

To preshrink cotton batting, gently soak it and allow to air dry before using. It also requires closer quilting, with rows of stitches spaced every 1" to 2" to keep it in place.

Remove the batting from the package 24 hours before it is to be used to allow it to relax. Smooth it out on a bed or table to unwrinkle and fluff. If batting stays wrinkled after the relaxation period, don't use it.

Batting should be several inches larger all around than the finished quilt top. If necessary, you can enlarge batting by cutting a strip the required width and butting the two pieces together. Secure with whipstitching.

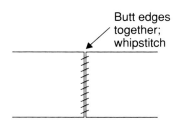

Butt edges together; whipstitch

Preparing the Quilt for the Frame

Select the backing for the quilt and seam it, if necessary. If you are using 44"-wide fabric, consult the following chart for the approximate yardage required for your quilt size.

Backing Yardage	
Quilt Size	**Amount of 44"-wide Fabric**
Baby (45" x 60")	1½ yds.
Twin (72" x 90")	5½ yds.
Full (81" x 96")	6 yds.
Queen (90" x 108")	10 yds.
King (120" x 120")	10½ yds.

When piecing the backing, plan it so seams are in the center. For larger quilts, center one fabric width and add the required additional width at each side to make the backing. Press seams open. Allow an extra 4" of backing fabric all around the quilt so the fabric can give during the quilting process.

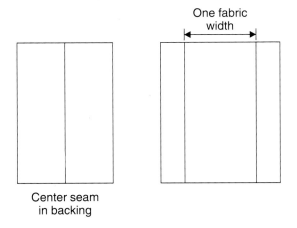

One fabric width

Center seam in backing

Working on a large, flat surface, layer the quilt with the backing face down on the bottom, then the batting, and finally the quilt top. Hand baste the layers together as shown, at right, or pin the layers together with small, rustproof safety pins. Pin every 6", starting from the center and working out to the edges of the quilt. If necessary, carefully roll the quilt to reach the center. Then unroll as you work, constantly checking underneath for wrinkles.

Batting   Backing

To hand baste the quilt, pin the layers together every 12" to keep the quilt from shifting. Place the quilt on a large table and roll one side toward the center. Begin basting toward yourself, smoothing, unpinning, and unrolling the quilt as you baste. Roll the quilt up again and baste another row 4" away from the first. Repeat basting until half of the quilt is basted. Turn the quilt and baste the remaining half in the same manner.

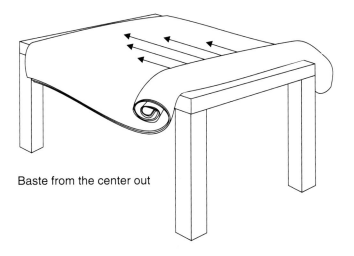

Baste from the center out

Quilting Frames

You may hand quilt the layers together, working in a lap hoop or frame or in a floor frame. My favorite frame is the Q-Snap. It is made of plastic PVC pipe that just snaps on and off the quilt with ease. It also prevents stretching during quilting. The quilt will be rather loose, but without wrinkles in the frame or hoop, as quilting is best done with the layers under *slightly* loose tension. This prevents bent and broken quilting needles. It is also easier to make small quilting stitches when the quilt is held under loose rather than too-tight tension in the quilting frame.

To lap quilt a large quilt, fold the quilt toward the center from all four edges so it is a more manageable size. Always start quilting from the center out, removing the basting or safety pins as you go.

If you plan to use a floor frame, basting or pinning the layers together is optional. If the quilt layers are carefully handled, you can stretch them directly onto the frame. It usually requires at least two people to mount a quilt on a floor frame.

1. Attach and roll one side of the quilt up and over the rails. Repeat with the opposite side of the quilt. About one yard in the center of the quilt will be exposed and that will be quilted first.

2. After quilting the center, roll and unroll to one end and then to the other to finish the quilt.

Where to Quilt

There are several ways to quilt. The following are two methods particularly suited to beginning quilters. As your skills improve, you may choose more elaborate patterns, found in a number of quilt pattern books.

"Stitch-in-the-ditch" quilting stitches follow right next to the seam lines on the side where there are no seam allowances. (The seams have been pressed to one side.) This method emphasizes the patchwork design.

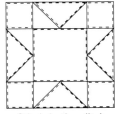

Stitch in the ditch

In "selective quilting," the patchwork is quilted "in the ditch" and across the blocks. This is done to unify or simplify the surface of a busy or complicated quilt top. To mark lines across the blocks where there are no seam lines to follow, use ¼"-wide masking tape, taping each block just before you're ready to stitch. Remove tape immediately to avoid leaving a tape residue.

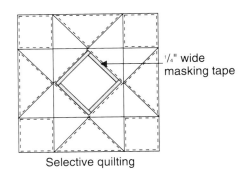

¼" wide masking tape

Selective quilting

Do not leave areas larger than 4" wide unquilted. Try to quilt the entire surface of the quilt with the same density of stitches whenever possible to prevent distortion.

When quilting across areas containing many layers of fabric (such as star centers and corners), slow down the quilting process, taking one stitch at a time and working to carefully match the length of the previous quilting stitches.

The Quilting Stitch

The quilting stitch is an important part of the overall appearance of the quilt. A little practice will make it easy.

Use quilting thread or cotton thread coated with beeswax. A quilting needle is called a "Between" and is available in sizes from 5 to 12. The larger the number, the smaller the needle. For more control and smaller stitches, use the smallest needle that is comfortable for you to thread and handle.

1. Thread the needle directly from the spool. This avoids tangles and keeps the twist of the thread going in the right direction. After threading the needle, pull out 18" to 24" of the thread. Clip and make a small knot at the clipped end. Use a single strand of thread to quilt. If you do not knot your thread, begin in the same manner as you would with a knot. When you

take your first quilting stitch, use a backstitch to lock your thread in place.

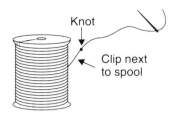

Knot

Clip next to spool

2. Start quilting from the center. The quilting stitch is a simple running stitch of 6 to 10 stitches per inch. Insert the needle into the quilt top approximately 1" from the place you wish to begin. Run the needle under the top and through the batting. Be careful not to catch the backing yet.

Bring the needle up where the first quilting stitch begins. Pull the thread, gently tugging the knot through the top so it becomes buried in the batting. Take a backstitch to secure the knot. By gently rocking the sewing hand, you can pack two or three stitches onto the needle. Push the needle to the surface and pull the thread firmly but not too tight.

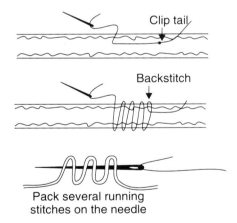

Clip tail

Backstitch

Pack several running stitches on the needle

Note: You will want to use a thimble on the middle finger of your sewing hand while quilting. It should not be too loose or too tight. The fingertip should just touch the end of the thimble. (Sometimes flattening the edge of the thimble helps.) A little experimenting will help you find the best stitching position.

3. With the sewing hand above the quilt and the non-sewing hand underneath, begin the quilting. Push the needle through so it just touches the index or middle finger on the underside of the quilt. With the thumb on your sewing hand, gently depress the surface of the quilt just ahead of the planned sewing area before bringing the needle back toward the surface.

Sew along the quilting line, working to make stitches of equal length. This may require concentration in the beginning, but it will flow as you gain experience. Eventually, you will develop your own stitching technique.

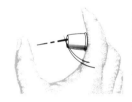

Push down in the fabric with the sewing-hand thumb in front of needle to get smaller stitches. Use thimble to push needle.

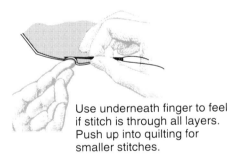

Use underneath finger to feel if stitch is through all layers. Push up into quilting for smaller stitches.

4. To end the stitch and secure the thread, take two back stitches and run the thread through the batting. Leave a tail in the center of your quilt sandwich so it will not work out during washing.

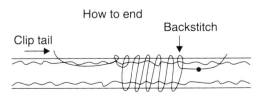

How to end

Clip tail

Backstitch

Quilting Tips

- To move from one quilted line to another, float the needle and thread through the inside layers of the quilt to the next location where you wish to stitch.

- When quilting curves or going through thick corners, quilt fewer stitches at a time. Take care to space them evenly so these stitches match the rest of the quilting. Evenly spaced stitches are more important than tiny ones when you're learning.

- Be sure to use the thimble to push the needle through the quilt. It helps avoid unnecessary twisting and turning, which cause tangles.

- Sometimes the finger under the quilt is poked with the needle point just a little too often. Quilters use many different methods to avoid this prick. Some use a plastic finger guard, some a leather thimble, some hold a spoon, some paint their fingertips with clear nail polish, and some learn to avoid the prick altogether.

- Try to quilt in a comfortable position, turning the work so the quilting moves from one side to the other and from top to bottom. Use good lighting and sit in a comfortable position. Try not to "tense up" your body. Rest the side of your quilting hand on the quilt to steady it. Now enjoy! Hand quilting can be quite calming and restful.

Using the "Quilt-As-You-Go" Method

If you find it easier to quilt each block before joining the blocks into a quilt top, you can use the "quilt-as-you-go" method. You will need a lap quilting frame.

1. To prepare the block for the frame, layer the completed block with muslin backing and the quilt batting and pin the layers together with extra-long, ball-headed pins.

2. Adjust the lap quilting frame to approximately the same size as the block. Tighten the screws on one corner. Pin the lattice to the frame along the edge of the canvas, adjusting the frame as you pin. Tighten the corners as the block is secured. The block should not be too tight as it will be harder to quilt. Remove the pins from the center of the quilt block as you work. By the time the block is secured in the frame, all pins should be removed from the block.

   Note: If a Q-Snap frame is used, eliminate the pinning. The 17" x 17" size works for most blocks. Adjust the blocks to fit the frame by basting muslin strips along the edges of the block, so it will fit in the lap frame. Remove the muslin strips after the block is quilted.

3. Quilt the block but do not quilt the last 2" along the outside edges of each block. This allows you to add blocks and borders with ease.

To assemble quilted blocks into a quilt top:

1. Trim batting and backing even with the block. Pin the batting and backing out of the way and sew the sides of the block with right sides together.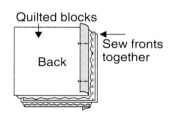

2. Whipstitch the edges of the batting together so that it lies flat. (It may be necessary to trim a little more from the batting edges before whipstitching for a smooth, flat joining.)

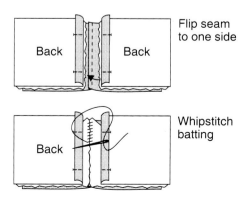

3. Do not seam the back yet. Lay one side of the backing flat and flip the other side of the backing out of the way. Quilt from the top as shown, ending quilting ½" short of the edges so that the blocks can be joined. You may want to unthread the quilting needle and leave the thread hanging free, then rethread when the blocks are joined, so you can complete the quilting across the corners of the blocks.

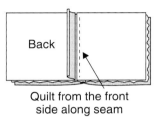

Quilt from the front
side along seam

4. Now turn under ¼" along the remaining edge of backing; slipstitch in place along the quilting.

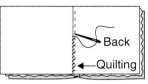

Whipstitch along quilting

5. Continue in same manner until all blocks are joined.

Tying a Comforter

Tying is a speedy alternative to hand quilting. A thicker batting (½"–¾") is usually used for tying a puffy comforter.

1. Prepare the quilt for tying by layering the quilt top, batting, and backing on a table or the floor. Secure carefully with rustproof safety pins spaced every 12" or so.

2. For the easiest tying method, use a chenille needle and cotton crochet thread. Use a double length of this heavy thread and do not knot the end.

3. Start at the center of the quilt. Tie by taking a ½"-long stitch through all 3 layers of the quilt. Wrap the thread around one hand and pick up the tail with that hand. Let the thread slip off the hand holding the tail, then tie an overhand knot. Wrap that hand again and finish the knot. Clip both ends even (about ½" long) and proceed to the next area to tie.

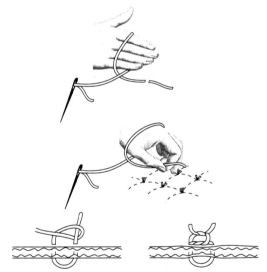

Option: Use a large darning needle and yarn to tie the quilt. Embroidery floss, candlewick yarn, or ¹⁄₁₆"-wide ribbon are other options for the "ties." Use a needle that is a little larger than the tie material. The eye of the needle must accommodate the "tie" thickness.

Binding

When the quilting is completed and the basting has been removed, it's time to bind the edges of the quilt.

1. Trim the batting and backing even with the edges of the quilt top.

2. Cut 2½"-wide bias strips for the durable, double-folded binding. Cut enough strips to go around the quilt, plus an extra 12" or so. Seam the strips on the diagonal; trim seams to ¼" and press open as shown.

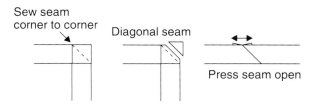

Fold the binding in half, wrong sides together. Press, taking care not to stretch the bias. Then, open out the binding and trim one end at a 45° angle. Turn under and press ¼" as shown.

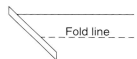

3. Beginning a few inches in from one corner of the quilt, pin the pressed binding to the quilt top, matching the raw edges. Stitch the binding to the quilt by machine, using a ¼"-wide seam.

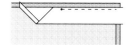

Right side of quilt

4. Stop stitching ¼" from the first corner and backstitch to secure.

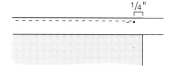

Fold the binding back diagonally at a 45° angle.

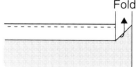

Then, flip the binding down, even with the edge of the quilt.

Start sewing the binding ¼" from the corner, securing with backstitching.

Repeat with remaining corners.

5. When you reach the beginning of the binding strip, overlap the beginning stitching about 1". Then, trim the excess binding at a 45° angle and tuck into the beginning of the binding.

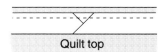

6. Fold the binding around to the back of the quilt. A folded miter will appear on the front of the quilt. On the back, fold one side, then the other to create the miter on the back. Stitch the folded edge of the binding to the back of the quilt by hand.

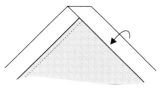

Wrong side of quilt

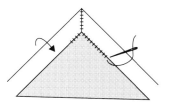

Kansas Sampler Quilts

"Primary Sampler" is a Kansas Sampler Variation, featuring the Virginia Robertson Collection. The 2" lattices, 2" corners, and 6" border embrace 12" blocks to finish at 66" x 93".

The Kansas Sampler is actually the culmination of sixteen years of teaching experience. The quilt is taught as a Block-of-the-Month project, giving the quilting student the opportunity to learn new techniques each month with time between classes to practice each skill while making blocks for a quilt.

Over the years, I've developed five different Block-of-the-Month quilts and have found that no matter how many times they are made, the quilts are never the same. Individual interpretation, improved sewing techniques, different color combinations, and exciting fabrics continually restate that "basic can be beautiful." The following Kansas Sampler Quilt variations are uniquely different, yet the basic blocks are the same. Follow the color scheme shown or plan your own color scheme and purchase fabrics, referring to Fabric Requirements for Sampler Blocks.

Kansas Sampler with Piano Key Border

The "Kansas Sampler with Piano Key Border," a 73½" x 85½" coverlet, demonstrates the significance of color choice and block positioning. The addition of a piano key border creates a frame for the central blocks.

Finished Size: *73½" x 85½"*

All the Kansas Sampler blocks, except the Grandmother's Fan, were used for this sweet, Victorian sampler. The center is pieced as a medallion, and the outer border is a "Piano Key" design that uses up the scraps.

Materials: *44"-wide fabric*

Note: Yardages are given only for lattice, borders, and backing. Yardage for quilt blocks will vary, depending on the blocks you make for your quilt and how you want to use the fabrics within them.

*2½ yds. for lattices and inner and outer
 borders
1¾ yds. total assorted darks for piano keys
1¾ yds. total assorted lights for piano keys
5½ yds. for backing
Batting, binding, and thread to finish*

Cutting: *All strips are cut across fabric width (crosswise grain).*
1. From the lattice fabric, cut:
     2 strips, each 2½" x 24½"
     4 strips, each 2½" x 12½"
     4 strips, each 2½" x 44"
     Piece together, end to end, and cut 2
     strips, each 2½" x 64½".
2. From the assorted dark and light fabrics for the piano keys, cut a total of 20 light strips and 20 dark strips, each 2" wide.

Make the Sampler Blocks
1. Plan your color scheme and purchase fabrics, following the guidelines on color and fabric selection beginning on page 8.
2. Following the directions for the Kansas Sampler blocks on the pages indicated, make the following:

     4 Log Cabin blocks—page 22
     2 Crazy Quilt blocks—page 34

2 Dresden Plate blocks—page 29
2 Pieced Blocks with Half-Square Tri-
    angles in 16-Patch Grids—page 21
4 Ninepatch blocks—page 20
1 Eight-Pointed Star—page 14
3 Hourglass blocks—page 20
2 String blocks, each 13" square, then
    cut in fourths—page 26

Assemble the Quilt Top

Note: Refer to the numbered illustration below, which is keyed to the following steps.

1. Join the 4 Log Cabin blocks with the dark sides in the center.
2. Add 4 String blocks, arranged zigzag fashion, to the top and to the bottom of the Log Cabin medallion.
3. Stitch the 2½" x 24½" lattice strips to the top and bottom edges of the panel.
4. Add 2 of the remaining pieced blocks to the top and 2 to the bottom edge to complete the central panel.
5. Assemble 2 side panels, using the remaining pieced blocks and 4 lattice strips, each 2½" x 12½".
6. Join side panels to central panel with 2½" x 64½" lattice strips.

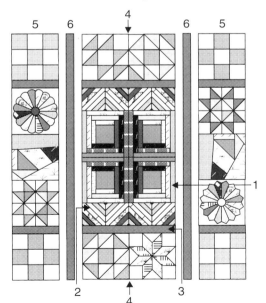

Make the Piano Key Border

1. Piece the piano key strips into 4 units of ten 2" strips, each with light and dark alternating. As you add a strip, alternate the

sewing direction to prevent the finished unit from curving and distorting.

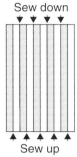

Sew down
Sew up
Alternate sewing directions

2. Crosscut the strip-pieced units into 6"-wide segments, checking to make sure that each segment is "true" before cutting. You will probably find it necessary to true up an edge of each segment as you cut, cutting away ⅛" to ¼" on one side to keep the segments squared.

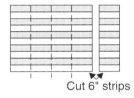

Cut 6" strips

3. Join the strip-pieced units to make 2 border strips, each 6" x 73½", for the top and bottom and 2 border strips, each 6" x 85½" for the sides. These are cut a little long to allow for easy mitering. (See Mitered Borders, page 39).
4. From the remaining lattice fabric, cut 2 border strips, each 3" x 73½", and 2 strips, each 3" x 85½". Stitch a border strip to each long edge of each piano-key border strip. Press both seams in the same direction.

2½" strips
6" Piano Keys
2½" strips

5. Attach the borders, following the directions for Mitered Borders on page 39.

Complete the Quilt

1. Layer the quilt top with batting and backing. Baste.
2. Quilt as desired and bind the edges.

Quilter's Thimble Sampler

Finished Size: *79½" x 111½"*

This sampler uses many of the basic designs in a unique way. The outside border is an interesting stripe that helps pull the quilt together. The center looks like a medallion, but it is sashed with corner blocks in the traditional way. The value contrast in the Log Cabin and String blocks creates the dramatic, on-point center.

Materials: *44"-wide fabric*

Note: Yardages are given only for lattice, lattice corner blocks, borders, and backing. Yardage for quilt blocks will vary, depending on the blocks you make for your quilt and how you want to use the fabrics within them. See below.

⅜ yd. for lattice corner blocks
2⅞ yds. for lattice strips
3 yds. lengthwise stripe for border*
8 yds. for backing
Batting, binding, and thread to finish
* You may use a crosswise stripe if you wish, but it will be necessary to piece the border strips.

Cutting: *All strips are cut across fabric width (crosswise grain).*
1. From the fabric for the lattice corner blocks, cut two 4½"-wide strips. Crosscut 15 squares, each 4½" x 4½".
2. From the lattice fabric, cut 22 strips, each 4½" wide. From 13 of these strips, cut 38 short lattice strips, each 4½" x 12½". From the remaining strips, cut and piece the following:
    2 strips, each 4½" x 68½" (top and bottom lattice)
    2 strips, each 4½" x 92½" (side lattice)

Make the Sampler Blocks
1. Plan your color scheme and purchase fabrics for your blocks, following the guidelines beginning on page 8.
2. Following the directions for the Kansas Sampler blocks on the pages indicated, make the following:

8 Log Cabin blocks—page 22
4 String blocks—page 26
4 Ninepatch blocks—page 12
8 Pieced Blocks with Half-Square Triangles in Ninepatch grids—page 18

Assemble the Quilt Top
1. Referring to the diagram, assemble the blocks with lattices and corner blocks. See Lattices with Corner Blocks on page 37.

2. Add the longest lattice strips (4½" x 92½") to the sides and then the remaining lattice strips (4½" x 68") to the top and bottom edges of the quilt top.
3. Cut 6"-wide border strips from the striped border fabric, following directions for Mitered Borders on page 39. Sew borders to quilt, mitering the corners as shown.

Note: Adjust the width of the border strips to the width of the stripe if necessary. If cut wider than 6", border strips will need to be cut longer, and you may need additional yardage.

Complete the Quilt
1. Layer the quilt top with batting and backing. Baste.
2. Quilt as desired and bind the edges.

Two quilt shop owners, Carol Jacobs and Kathy Schwartz, from "The Quilter's Thimble" in Freeport, Illinois, came to the Quilt Factory for a visit and discovered the "Kansas Sampler." They left saying, "Yes, we could do that!" and they did! Less than a month after their visit, the finished 79½" x 111½" "Quilter's Thimble Quilt" arrived by mail for a show-and-tell.

Kansas Sampler with Flying Geese Border

Finished Size: *78½" x 106½"*

The shaded center square in this vividly colored quilt is set on point and was created with carefully colored String and Log Cabin blocks. Flying Geese borders made from half-square triangle blocks add the finishing touch and lots of movement.

Materials: *44"-wide fabric*

Note: Yardages are given only for lattice, lattice corner blocks, borders, and backing. Yardage for quilt blocks will vary, depending on the blocks you make for your quilt and how you want to use the fabrics within them. See below.

¼ yd. for lattice corner blocks
1½ yds. for lattice strips
⅜ yd. for narrow inner border
½ yd. for outer border
8 yds. for backing
Batting, binding, and thread to finish

Cutting: *All strips are cut across fabric width (crosswise grain).*
1. For the corner blocks, cut two 2½"-wide strips. Crosscut 35 squares, 2½" x 2½".
2. For the lattice strips, cut twenty 2½"-wide strips. Crosscut 58 strips, each 2½" x 12½".
3. For the narrow inner border, cut eight 1½"-wide strips.
4. For the outer border, cut nine 1½"-wide strips.

Make the Sampler Blocks
1. Plan your color scheme and purchase fabrics, following the guidelines on color and fabric selection beginning on page 8.
2. Following the directions for the Kansas Sampler blocks on the pages indicated, make the following:
   4 Ninepatch blocks—page 12
   8 Log Cabin blocks—page 22
   4 String blocks—page 26
   8 Pieced Blocks with Half-Square Triangles in Ninepatch grids—page 18

Assemble the Quilt Top
1. Referring to the quilt photo, assemble the blocks with lattices and corner blocks. See Lattices with Corner Blocks on page 37.
2. Piece and sew inner border strips to the sides of the quilt top, following the directions for Straight-Cut Borders on page 39. Repeat with top and bottom border strips.

Make the Flying Geese Borders
1. Make 148 half-square triangle blocks for the Flying Geese borders, using a grid sized for 4" finished blocks (page 18) and assorted fabrics from your selection. Make an additional 16 half-square triangle blocks for the border corner blocks and set aside for step 4, on page 54.

2. Stitch the half-square triangle blocks together in pairs as shown to create the Flying Geese border units.

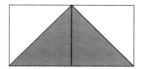

3. Join the Flying Geese units into borders. Make 2 border strips, each containing 22 units, for the sides and make 2 border strips, each containing 15 units, for the top and bottom.

"Kansas Sampler with Flying Geese Border" measures 78½" x 106½" and features fabrics from the Virginia Robertson Collection by Fabri-Quilt. Originally the quilt was made as a sample to introduce the new fabric line.

4. Assemble 4 corner blocks, using 16 half-square triangle blocks set aside earlier. Sew these corner blocks to both ends of the top and bottom Flying Geese borders.

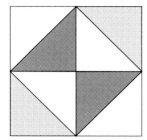

5. Sew the Flying Geese borders to the sides of the quilt. Then sew the top and bottom Flying Geese borders with corner blocks to the quilt.

1 1/2" strips

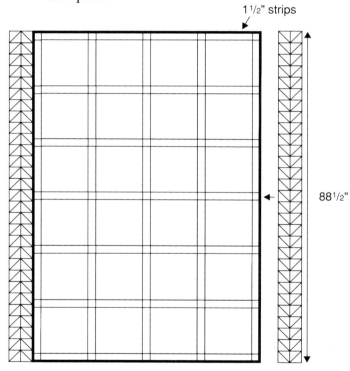

88 1/2"

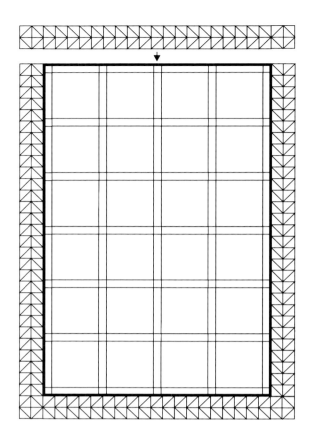

Complete the Quilt
1. Sew the outer side borders to the quilt and then add the top and bottom borders.
2. Layer the quilt top with batting and backing. Baste.
3. Quilt as desired and bind the edges.

Primary Sampler

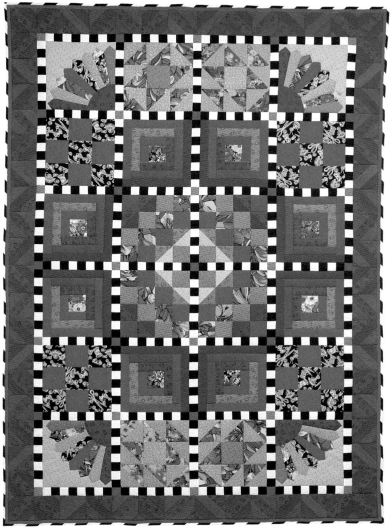

"Primary Sampler" is another Kansas Sampler Variation, featuring the Virginia Robertson Collection. The 2" lattices, 2" corners, and 6" borders embrace 12" blocks to finish at 66" x 93".

Finished Size: *66" x 93"*

This contemporary sampler quilt was created using the color-wheel graphics from the "Virginia Robertson" fabric collection, produced by Fabri-Quilt and a black-and-white stripe for the lattices. The surface just vibrates with optical interest.

Materials: *44"-wide fabric*

Note: Yardages are given only for lattice, borders, and backing. Yardage for quilt blocks will vary, depending on the blocks you make for your quilt and how you want to use the fabrics within them.

1⅛ yds. black-and-white stripe for lattice strips*
assorted fabric scraps from blocks for lattice corner blocks
⅓ yd. for outer border
6 yds. for backing
1 yd. black-and-white stripe for bias binding
Batting and thread to finish

* *Stripes should be 1½" wide for best results. Stripes ¾" wide will also work well.*

Cutting: *All strips (except bias binding) are cut across the fabric width (crosswise grain).*

1. From the black-and-white stripe, cut nineteen 2"-wide strips (cutting across the stripes). Crosscut into 58 lattice strips, each 2" x 12½".
2. From the fabric for the lattice corner blocks, cut 35 squares, each 2" x 2".
3. From the outer border fabric, cut nine 1"-wide strips.
4. From the stripe for the binding, cut 3"-wide bias strips and piece together to make a continuous strip of bias binding.

   Note: This width binding strip will finish to ½" when doubled and attached to the quilt, using a ½"-wide seam.

Make the Sampler Blocks
1. Plan your color scheme and purchase fabrics, following the guidelines beginning on page 8.
2. Following the directions for the Kansas Sampler blocks on the pages indicated, make the following:

   4 Grandmother's Fan blocks—page 32
   4 Double X blocks based on a
      Ninepatch Grid—page 20
   4 Ninepatch blocks—page 12
   8 Log Cabin blocks—page 22
   4 Pieced Blocks based on a 16-patch
      grid—page 21

Make String Blocks for Middle Border
1. To make 56 String Blocks that will finish to 4½" square, cut fourteen 10"-square paper foundations. Piece the String blocks on the paper, following the directions on page 26. In addition, make 8 String blocks in the same manner, but piece them on 11"-square paper foundations.
2. Cut 4 blocks, each 5" square, from the 10" pieced blocks, and 4 blocks, each 5½" square, from the 11" pieced blocks.

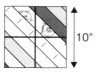

Piece fourteen 10" blocks. Cut into 4 blocks each, for 56 total.

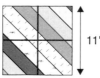

Piece two 11" blocks. Cut into 4 blocks each, for 8 total.

Note: Be sure to leave the paper on the blocks until the quilt top is assembled and borders have been attached.

3. Measure the length of the quilt at the center to determine the required length of the String-block border. Piece 5"-square String blocks together to create side borders, using 2 of the 5½" String blocks in the center of the border strip and trimming them to the correct size so the finished border will measure the correct length. Repeat for the top and bottom String-block borders. Side borders should have 18 String blocks in each, and top and bottom borders should have 14 String blocks in each.

Center blocks must be
custom cut from 5½" blocks

Assemble the Quilt Top
1. Referring to the quilt photo, assemble the blocks with lattices and corner blocks. See Lattices with Corner Blocks on page 37.
2. Attach the String-block borders to the sides and then to the top and bottom of the quilt top.
3. Add the outer border, following the directions for Straight-Cut Borders on page 39.

Complete the Quilt
1. Layer the quilt top with batting and backing. Baste.
2. Quilt as desired and bind the edges with the striped bias binding, using ½"-wide seams so finished binding is ½" wide.

C-27
Spin-Off Quilts

Fabric collecting is considered normal behavior around the Quilt Factory. Quilters collect fabrics in a variety of colors and designs. Fabric is to the quilter what paint is to the painter. I've owned a quilt shop for ten years, and my personal fabric collection has reached epic proportions. My love for surface design has grown as well. When Fabri-Quilt asked me to design a fabric line for quilters in 1991, my imagination reeled with the potential.

Pinning up quilts in progress lets you step back and take a look.

The Virginia Robertson Fabric Collection is spread out on a work table to make fabric choices easier.

Having an entire new color and pattern palette opened the door to all kinds of design possibilities. I decided to include fabrics in shaded gradations for the slightest suggestion of a color change. Bright prints in colors straight from the color wheel with solids to match are available as a result. These fabrics just call out to be used in wonderful quilts. When fabrics in my first collection of designs arrived, everyone at the Quilt Factory was thrilled. And, everyone wanted to do something with them. So, we did!

Experimenting with new fabric is fun as the wheels start turning. After teaching several versions of the Kansas Sampler Quilt for the past sixteen years, I found it easy to use the idea as a point of departure, incorporating the new fabric line. This was the start of a series of designs we call "Spin-Off" quilts. A "Spin-Off" simply takes a known technique and pushes it as far as possible.

Actually, it all started with one over-achieving student who took my beginning quilting class many years ago. During each class in the series, I taught how to make a new block, incorporating new quilting techniques with the idea that the student would make a few blocks for her sampler quilt. This particular student would return for the next class with an entire quilt top done in that technique! Before we were done, she not only had quite a collection of quilt tops, but also a vast knowledge of color and design. And, she had fun!

The staff started their "Spin-Offs" by choosing a block from the Kansas Sampler and developing it further. The designs are traditional but the manner of arriving at the finished quilt may not be. We used half-square triangle grid sheets, rotary cutters, strip piecing, paste-up blocks, and a little serendipity to create the fun in these colorful quilts.

Irish Ninepatch

"Irish Ninepatch" utilizes Helen Crook's unique approach to make this 84½" x 96½" Irish Ninepatch a quick quilt.

Finished Size: *84½" x 96½"*

The "Irish Ninepatch" variation consists of two different Ninepatch blocks, using five colors. Depending on how you look at the lively surface of this quilt, you can see an Irish Chain, Four Patch blocks, or woven chains of color. Select a light solid, two light prints, a dark/medium print, and a dark print.

This quilt makes a queen-size comforter or a bedspread for a double bed. To make the quilt larger, add extra Ninepatch blocks or outer borders as desired.

Materials: *44"-wide fabric*
2¼ yds. light solid
1¼ yds. light red print
2¼ yds. light blue print
1⅔ yds. medium red print
2⅔ yds. dark blue print
Backing, batting, binding, and thread to finish

Cutting: *All strips are cut across fabric width (crosswise grain).*

Cut the number of 2½"-wide strips from each fabric as indicated:

Light solid: 28 strips

Light red: 14 strips
Light blue: 28 strips
Medium red: 21 strips
Dark blue: 35 strips

Directions

1. To each of 14 light solid strips, stitch a medium red strip and a light red strip. Press seams away from the light solid strip. Crosscut strip-pieced units into 2½"-wide segments.

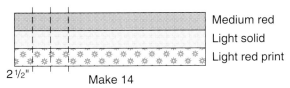

Medium red
Light solid
Light red print

2½" Make 14

2. Sew a light solid strip to each long edge of 7 medium red strips. Press seams away from the light strip. Crosscut into 2½"-wide segments.

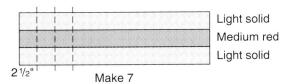

Light solid
Medium red
Light solid

2½" Make 7

3. Piece 112 red Ninepatch blocks.

Make 112

4. Sew a dark blue strip to each long edge of 14 light blue strips. Press seams away from the dark blocks. Crosscut into 2½"-wide segments.

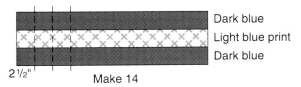

Dark blue
Light blue print
Dark blue

2½" Make 14

5. Sew a light blue strip to each long edge of 7 dark blue strips. Press seams away from the dark blocks. Crosscut into 2½"-wide segments.

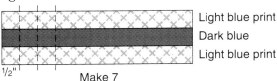

Light blue print
Dark blue
Light blue print

2½" Make 7

6. Piece 112 blue Ninepatch blocks.

Make 112

7. Working on a large, flat surface, lay out the blocks, referring to the quilt diagram, with 14 blocks across and 16 blocks down.

8. Stitch the blocks in the first row together and press the seams all in one direction, being careful not to disturb the pressing within the Ninepatch blocks.

9. Assemble the next row of blocks and press the seams in the opposite direction from the first row. Continue in the same manner until all rows are complete. Then, join rows together to create the quilt top.

10. Layer the quilt top with batting and backing. Baste.

11. Quilt as desired and bind the edges with the bias binding.

Twinkle, Twinkle, Little Star

Finished Size: *33½" x 46"*

"Twinkle, Twinkle, Little Star" is made of Star blocks, using the basic techniques described for the hand-pieced Eight-Pointed Star on page 14. If you look carefully, you will find two Six-Pointed Stars hidden amidst the rows of Tumbling Blocks. The same basic diamond shape is used for both; the placement of the light, medium, and dark fabrics determines whether it looks like a star or a block.

The quilt shown was made from fourteen different country Christmas fabrics in shades of cream, Turkey red, and forest green. In addition to the directions for the featured quilt, you will find directions for a quilt made of Six-Pointed Stars.

Before you begin your quilt, make plastic templates, using those found on page 64 and following the template-making directions on page 16.

Note: The Six-Pointed Star is made of diamonds cut from Template A. You will need Templates B, C, D, and E to complete the quilt top at the outer edges as indicated on the quilt plans that follow.

Choose a dark, a medium, and a light fabric for the blocks. By arranging these values in different ways, you can create Tumbling Blocks or Six-Pointed Stars.

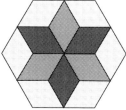

Six-Pointed Star

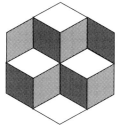

Tumbling Blocks

Allover Six-Pointed Star

Design options

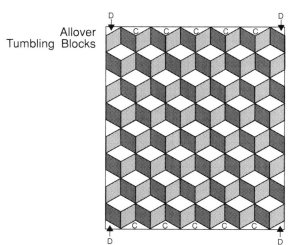

Allover Tumbling Blocks

Using the colors you've selected, make test blocks with paper paste-ups to check the fabric selection. The fabrics could be a mixed-up selection of scraps, if each fabric is categorized into the appropriate pile of light, medium, and dark.

Materials: *44"-wide fabric*
 ¼ yd. each of 4 different greens
 ¼ yd. each of 4 different reds
 ¼ yd. each of 6 to 8 light prints
 ⅓ yd. green for inner border*
 ¼ yd. red for middle border
 ¼ yd. green for outer border*
 Backing, batting, binding, and thread to finish

*In the quilt shown, the same green was used for the inner and outer borders, requiring ⅝ yard total, of a single fabric.

"Twinkle, Twinkle, Little Star" creates an optical illusion when the twinkling blocks become six-pointed stars, just by changing the color. This wall hanging measures 33½" x 46".

Cutting

1. Using Template A, cut:
   59 diamonds from assorted lights
   52 diamonds from assorted reds
   52 diamonds from assorted greens
2. Using Template B, cut 10 half diamonds from assorted lights.
3. Using Template C, cut 11 long half diamonds from the green for inner border.
4. Using Template D, cut 2 corners from the green fabric for the inner border.
5. From the inner border fabric, cut five 2½"-wide strips.
6. From the middle border fabric, cut five 1½"-wide strips.
7. From the outer border fabric, cut five 1½"-wide strips.

Directions

Note: The quilt shown in the color photo was constructed in a slightly different manner than the directions given here. Directions were modified after the quilt was made for easier piecing.

1. Working on a large, flat surface, lay out pieces, following the quilt plan below.

2. Assemble diamonds into pairs, then into sets of fours, and then into chains, begin-

ning and ending the seams at the seam intersections as shown.

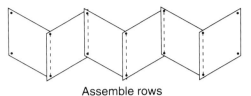

Assemble rows

3. Set in a diamond at the top of each block, carefully matching the seam allowance and pivoting at the set-in corners. Pinwheel-press the seams as shown.

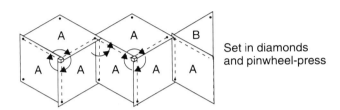

Set in diamonds and pinwheel-press

4. Sew the completed rows of blocks together to create the quilt top. Use Templates D and E to cut corners and pieces for the outer edges.
5. Following the directions on page 39 for measuring the quilt to determine border length for border strips, seam inner border strips together as necessary to make borders of the required lengths. Repeat with the middle and outer border strips. Stitch the 3 border strips together for each side of the quilt.

   Attach the borders to the quilt and miter corners.
6. Layer the quilt top with batting and backing. Baste.
7. Quilt as desired and bind the edges.

If you prefer to create a quilt top of Star blocks, use the following procedure to piece the blocks and assemble the quilt top.

1. Using Template A, cut 6 diamonds for each complete Star block from assorted medium and dark fabrics. Using Template A, cut 6 diamonds for each complete Star block from assorted lights for the background. In your quilt layout, you will also need half blocks. For each half block, cut 3 diamonds from assorted medium and dark fabrics and 3 diamonds from assorted light fabrics for the background.

2. Lay out the pieces for Star blocks in the desired arrangement and use Templates D and E to cut corners and pieces for the top and bottom edges where required. (See quilt plan below.)

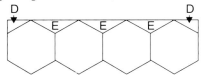

3. To assemble a Six-Pointed Star, hand piece 2 diamonds together, beginning and ending the seam at the marked seam intersections. With thread still attached, add the third diamond. Repeat with the remaining 3 diamonds.

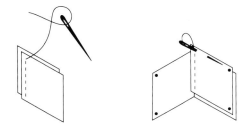

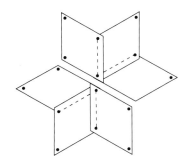

Sew the star halves together, being careful not to sew past the marked seam intersections to keep the seam allowances free for easier pressing.

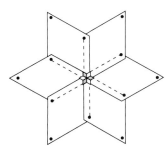

4. Pinwheel-press the star to make the center lie flat.

Note: If any of the stitches crossed the

seam intersections, the center will not lie flat. If there is a hole in the center of the star, you have not sewn to the marked seam intersection. Identify and correct these problems now.

5. Set in the corner diamonds, carefully matching the seam allowance and pivoting at the set-in corners. Pinwheel-press the seams as shown.

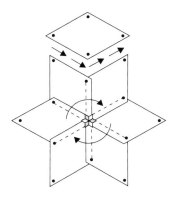

6. Arrange the blocks in rows and assemble, row by row, adding corners (Template D) and outer edge piece (Template E) as needed to complete the rows.
7. Join completed rows.

8. Layer the quilt top with batting and backing. Baste.
9. Quilt as desired and bind the edges.

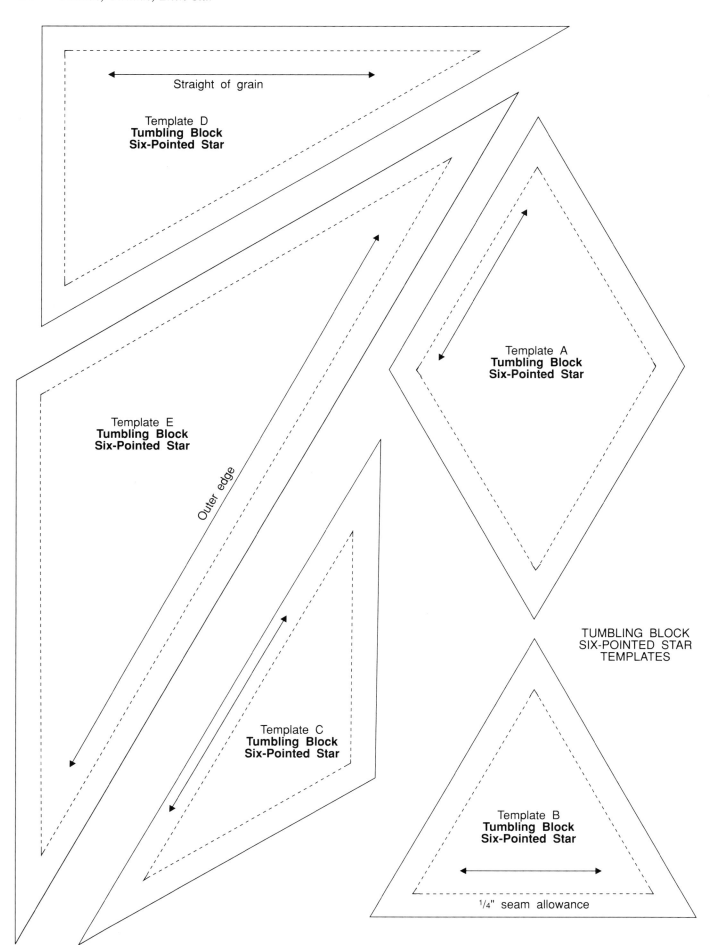

Straight of grain

Template D
**Tumbling Block
Six-Pointed Star**

Template A
**Tumbling Block
Six-Pointed Star**

Template E
**Tumbling Block
Six-Pointed Star**

Outer edge

TUMBLING BLOCK
SIX-POINTED STAR
TEMPLATES

Template C
**Tumbling Block
Six-Pointed Star**

Template B
**Tumbling Block
Six-Pointed Star**

¹/₄" seam allowance

Gradation Graphics— "Indonesian Sunrise"

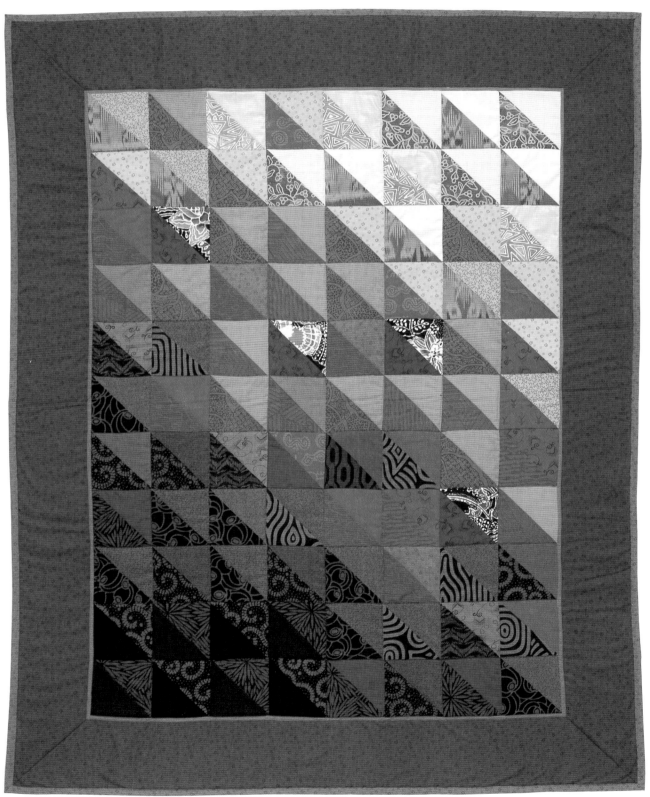

"Indonesian Sunrise" blends Bali fabrics along with vivid colors from the Virginia Robertson Fabric Collection to create these half-square triangle blocks and give the luminous 43" x 55" wall hanging a little extra zip.

"Indonesian Sunrise" and "Teal We Meet Again" are made of 4" finished, half-square triangles. Beginning with the deepest darks and continuing through the mediums to the lighter shades, the colors were placed to form a diagonal glow of color. You will need a minimum of eighteen different fabrics in dark to light values to create these quilts. The key to a successful color scheme is to recognize the overall value of the color in each fabric and to place it so that the colors "glow" as they move across the quilt. It helps to squint when arranging the color combinations.

Directions below are for "Indonesian Sunrise"; "Teal We Meet Again" is somewhat smaller and requires a little less yardage for the borders.

Materials: *44"-wide fabric*
> *¼ yd. each of 18 to 36 fabrics in a progressive color gradation*
> *1⅔ yds. solid-colored fabric for inner border**
> *1⅔ yds. for outer border**
> *Backing, batting, binding, and thread to finish*
> **Border yardages allow you to cut continuous border strips. You will need less yardage if you prefer to cut borders from the crosswise grain.*

Directions

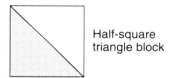

Half-square triangle block

1. Cut the paper grid sheet for 4" finished, half-square triangles (stapled in the center of this book) into 4- to 6-block units to create a variety of color combinations. As an alternative, cut, layer, and mark fabric with stitching and cutting grids for 4" finished, half-square triangles as shown on page 18.
2. Sew, cut, and press the half-square triangle blocks as directed. You will need a total of 88 blocks. You may want to make additional blocks for more design flexibility. Save the extras for another quilt project.
3. Work on a large, flat surface or a wall covered with batting or flannel and play with your blocks to create the design. Refer to the quilt photos on pages 65 and 67 for guidance in color placement.
4. Sew the first horizontal row of blocks together, using ¼"-wide seams; press all the seams in one direction.
5. Assemble the next row and press seams in the opposite direction from the pressing in the first row. Repeat this stitching and pressing sequence with remaining rows.
6. Assemble the rows, pinning the opposing seams, so they do not get twisted or pushed out of place during the sewing.
7. This quilt has 2 borders with mitered corners. Determine the finished outer dimensions of your quilt by measuring at the centers as shown on page 39 and adding 11" to each dimension for finished border width (5½" on each edge of the quilt). Cut the inner and outer border strips to match these dimensions, adding at least ½" for seam allowances to the length of each strip and cutting the inner border ¾" wide and the outer border 5½" wide.
8. Sew the inner and outer border strips together for each side of the quilt and press seams toward the outer border strip.

Press seams toward outer border strip

9. Attach borders to quilt as shown for Mitered Borders on page 39.
10. Layer the quilt top with batting and backing. Baste.
11. Quilt as desired and bind the edges.

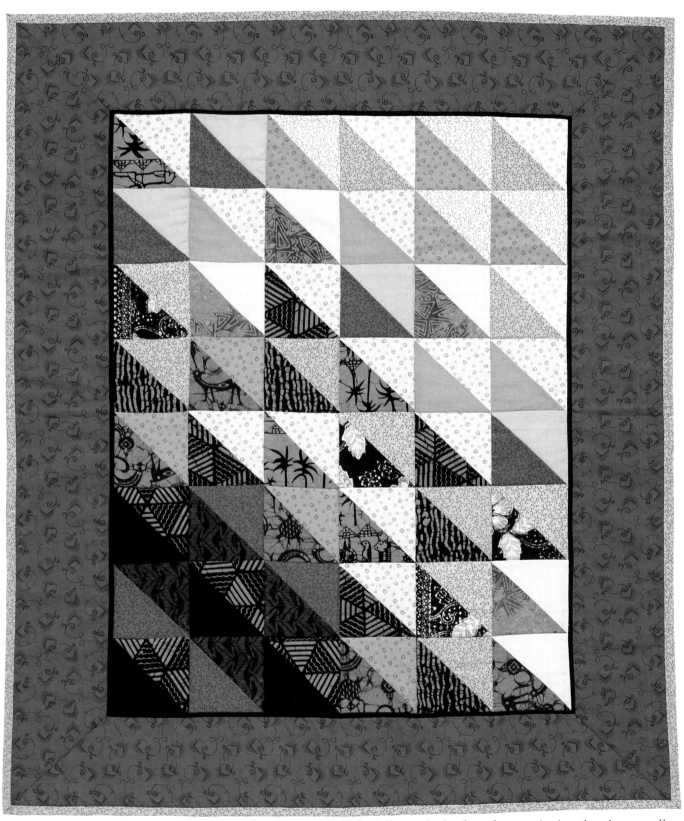

"Teal We Meet Again" uses the same half-square triangle blocks in different shades for a fun exercise in color play as well as producing a lovely 37½" x 45" wall hanging.

Triangle Trip around the World

Finished Size: *51" x 51"*

Like the Gradation Graphics quilts on pages 65 and 67, "Triangle Trip around the World" is made from 4" finished, half-square triangle blocks. We used fourteen different color combinations in this quilt with two value combinations—light/medium and medium/dark.

Materials: *44"-wide fabric*
> *1 fat quarter yd. each of 3 light prints**
> *1 fat quarter yd. each of 9 medium prints**
> *1 fat quarter yd. each of 5 dark prints and solids**
> *1¼ yds. for inner border***
> *1½ yds. for outer border***
> *Backing, batting, binding, and thread to finish*

*A fat quarter measures 18" x 22". If fat quarters are unavailable in your area, use ½ yards and share with a friend.

**Border yardages allow you to cut continuous border strips. You will need less yardage if you prefer to cut borders from the crosswise grain.

Directions

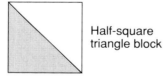

Half-square
triangle block

1. Use the paper grid sheet for 4" finished, half-square triangle blocks (stapled in the center of this book). Cut into 4 to 6 block units. As an alternative, cut, layer, and mark fabric with stitching and cutting grids for 4" finished, half-square triangle blocks as shown on page 18.
2. Sew, cut, and press the half-square triangle blocks as directed. You will need a total of 100 blocks in the following value combinations:
   > Light/Medium: Make 48
   > Medium/Dark: Make 52
3. Work on a large, flat surface or a wall covered with batting or flannel and play with your blocks to create the design, using 10 blocks down and 10 across. Refer to the quilt photo for color placement.
4. Sew the first horizontal row of blocks together, using ¼"-wide seams; press all the seams in one direction.
5. Assemble the next row and press seams in the opposite direction from the pressing in the first row. Repeat this stitching and pressing sequence with remaining rows.
6. Assemble the rows, pinning the opposing seams, so they do not get twisted or pushed out of place during the sewing.
7. This quilt has 2 borders with mitered corners. Determine the finished outer dimensions of your quilt by measuring at the centers as shown on page 39 and adding 11" to each dimension for finished border width (5½" on each edge of quilt). Cut the inner and outer border strips to match these dimensions, adding at least ½" for seam allowances to the length of each strip and cutting the inner border ¾" wide and the outer border 5½" wide.
8. Sew the inner and outer border strips together for each side of the quilt and press seams toward the outer border strip.

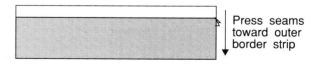

Press seams
toward outer
border strip

9. Attach borders to quilt as shown for Mitered Borders on page 39.
10. Layer the quilt top with batting and backing. Baste.
11. Quilt as desired and bind the edges.

"Triangle Trip around the World" is made in no time by using the 4" half-square triangle grid sheets found in the center of this book. Fabrics for this 51"-square quilt are from the Virginia Robertson Fabric Collection.

Peppermint Twist

Finished Size: *57" x 69"*

"Peppermint Twist" is made of 4" finished, half-square triangle blocks. You may vary the size by subtracting or adding more blocks as needed. For this quilt, you will need blocks made up in three sets of color values: (1) light pink and light green, (2) medium pink and dark red, (3) dark green and medium green.

Materials: *44"-wide fabric (prints and solids)*
  1 fat quarter yd. each of 4 light pinks*
  1 fat quarter yd. each of 4 medium pinks*
  1 fat quarter yd. each of 4 dark reds*
  1 fat quarter yd. each of 4 light greens*
  1 fat quarter yd. each of 4 medium greens*
  1 fat quarter yd. each of 4 dark greens*
  1⅝ yds. dark red solid for inner border**
  1⅝ yds. medium pink print for middle border**
  2 yds. dark red print for outer border**
  *Backing, batting, binding, and thread to
      finish*

*A fat quarter measures 18" x 22". If fat quarters are unavailable in your area, use ½ yards and share with a friend.

**Border yardages allow you to cut continuous border strips. You will need less yardage if you prefer to cut borders from the crosswise grain.

Directions

Half-square triangle block

1. Using the paper grid sheet for 4" finished, half-square triangle blocks (stapled in the center of this book), cut into 4- to 6-block units. As an alternative, cut, layer, and mark fabric with stitching and cutting grids for 4" finished, half-square triangle blocks as shown on page 18.
2. Sew, cut, and press the half-square triangle blocks as directed. You will need a total of 154 blocks in the following value combinations:
   Light Pink/Light Green: Make 51
   Medium Pink/Dark Red: Make 52
   Dark Green/Medium Green: Make 51
3. Work on a large, flat surface or a wall covered with batting or flannel and play with your blocks to arrange them into the quilt top, following the quilt photo as a guide for color placement. Use 11 blocks across and 14 down.
4. Sew the first horizontal row of blocks together, using ¼"-wide seams; press all the seams in one direction.
5. Assemble the next row and press seams in the opposite direction from the pressing in the first row. Repeat this stitching and pressing sequence with remaining rows.
6. Assemble the rows, pinning the opposing seams, so they do not get twisted or pushed out of place during the sewing.
7. This quilt has 3 borders with mitered corners. Determine the finished outer dimensions of your quilt by measuring at the centers as shown on page 39 and adding 13" to each dimension for finished border width (6½" on each edge of the quilt). Cut the inner and outer border strips to match these dimensions, adding at least ½" for seam allowances to the length of each strip and cutting them the widths indicated below:
   Inner border: ¾" wide
   Middle border: 1½" wide
   Outer border: 5½" wide
8. Sew the inner, middle, and outer border strips together for each side of the quilt and press seams toward the outer border strip.

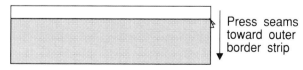
Press seams toward outer border strip

9. Attach borders to quilt as shown for Mitered Borders on page 39.
10. Layer the quilt top with batting and backing. Baste.
11. Quilt as desired and bind the edges.

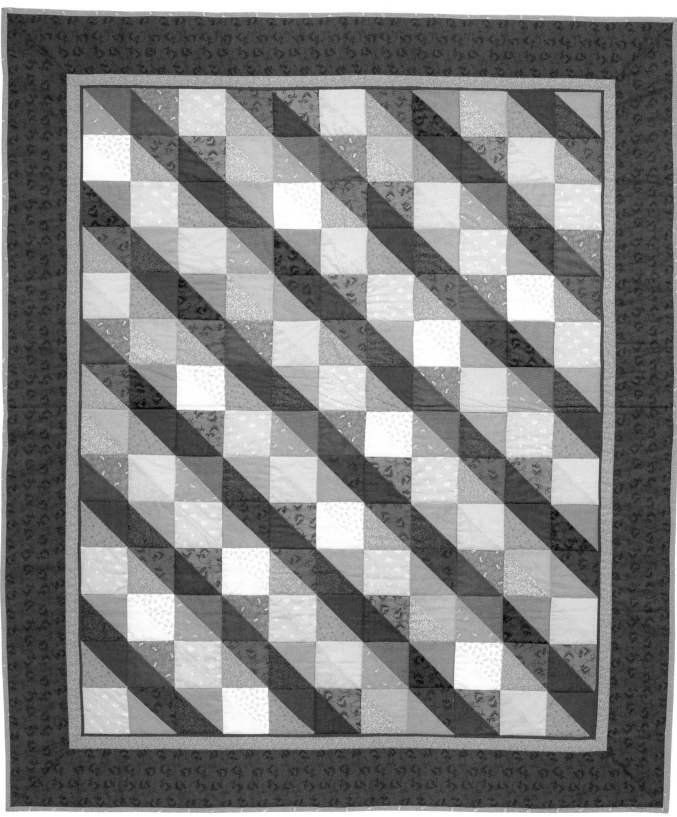

When Geri Cummings discovered Virginia Robertson's new fabrics, she immediately selected reds and greens. Geri devised the 57" x 69" "Peppermint Twist" quilt, using the half-square triangle grid sheets to make a quick wall hanging.

Grandmother's Fan

Finished Size: *39¼" x 48¼"*

Our "Grandmother's Fan" quilt is a traditional favorite. We have altered this spin-off from the sampler blocks, making the blocks 9", finished. The fan blades are smooth-ended rather than pointed like those in the sampler. This allows you to piece the background to the fan, eliminating hand appliqué as in the original block. Curved piecing takes its place.

In addition to the three borders surrounding the fan, we added a sashing strip on the left and bottom edge of the quilt to visually separate the fans from the borders.

Materials: *44"-wide fabric*
1 yd. light background
⅜ yd. accent color for quarter-circles*
¼ yd. each of 8 assorted prints for fan blades
¼ yd. for inner border
¼ yd. for middle border
1½ yds. for outer border
Backing, batting, binding, and thread to finish

*If you prefer, you may cut quarter-circles from assorted prints in the same color family as in the quilt shown in the photo.

Directions

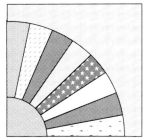
Grandmother's Fan

1. Make plastic templates of Templates A, B, and C on page 76, following the template-making directions on page 16.
2. For each block required, mark and cut 8 fan blades (Template A) from assorted prints; cut 1 background (Template B) and 1 center (Template C). Make 12 blocks.
3. Sew fan blades together in pairs, chain piecing on the machine for speedy sewing.

4. Clip the pairs apart and piece pairs into fours; then join sets of four into fans, each containing 8 fan blades. Press all seams in the same direction.

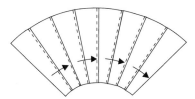
Press in one direction

5. Fold the quarter-circle in half and then in half again. Crease the folds firmly to mark the half- and quarter-points at the outer curved edges.

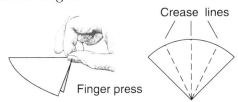
Finger press   Crease lines

6. Pin the outer curved edge of the quarter-circle to the inner curve of the fan, matching the center crease to the center seam and the quarter-point creases to the second and sixth seams.

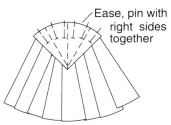
Ease, pin with right sides together

"Grandmother's Fan" sings of Tradition, Tradition! The 39¼" x 48¼" Grandmother's Fan continues to be a popular quilt.

7. Working with the fan side up, stitch the quarter-circle to the fan, easing into position as you sew. Piece by hand or machine. Press the seam toward the fan.

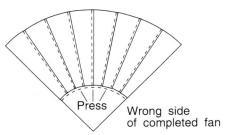

8. Fold the background piece in half and then in half again and finger-press to mark the half- and quarter-points.

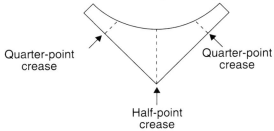

9. Pin the curved edge of the background piece to the outer curved edge of the fan, matching the center crease to the center seam and the quarter-point creases to the second and sixth seams. Be careful to match the seam intersections at the outer edges and pin securely.

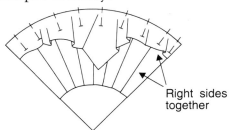

10. With the background piece on top, stitch, gently easing the edge of the background around the fan curve and removing pins as you reach them. Press seam toward fan.

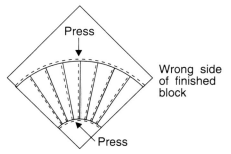

11. Arrange blocks 3 across and 4 down.
12. Sew the first horizontal row of blocks together, using ¼"-wide seams; press all the seams in one direction, being careful not to disturb the fan pressing within each of the blocks.
13. Assemble the next row of blocks and press seams in the opposite direction from the pressing in the first row. Repeat this stitching and pressing sequence with all remaining rows.
14. Assemble the rows, pinning the opposing seams so they do not get twisted or pushed out of place during the sewing.
15. Measure the length of the quilt top at the center and cut a 1½"-wide strip to that measurement. Stitch strip to the left-hand edge of the quilt top, easing as necessary.

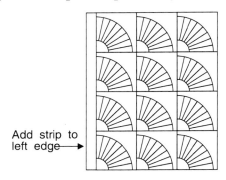

16. Measure the width of the quilt top across the center and cut a 1½"-wide strip to that measurement. Stitch strip to the bottom edge of the quilt top, easing as necessary.

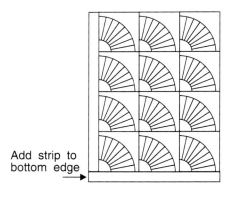

17. This quilt has 3 borders with mitered corners. Determine the finished outer dimensions of your quilt by measuring at the centers as shown on page 39 and adding 11¼" to each dimension for finished border width (5⅜" on each edge of the quilt).

Cut the inner, middle, and outer border strips to match these dimensions, adding at least ½" for seam allowances to the length of each strip and cutting them the widths indicated below:

Inner border: ⅞" wide
Middle border: 1½" wide
Outer border: 4½" wide

18. Sew the 3 border strips together for each side of the quilt and press seams toward the outer border strip.

Press seams toward outer border strip

19. Attach the borders to the quilt top as shown for Mitered Borders on page 39.
20. Layer the quilt top with batting and backing. Baste.
21. Quilt as desired and bind the edges.

Grandmother's Fan Quilt Plans

The quilt plans shown here are alternate layouts for larger quilts using the Grandmother's Fan block.

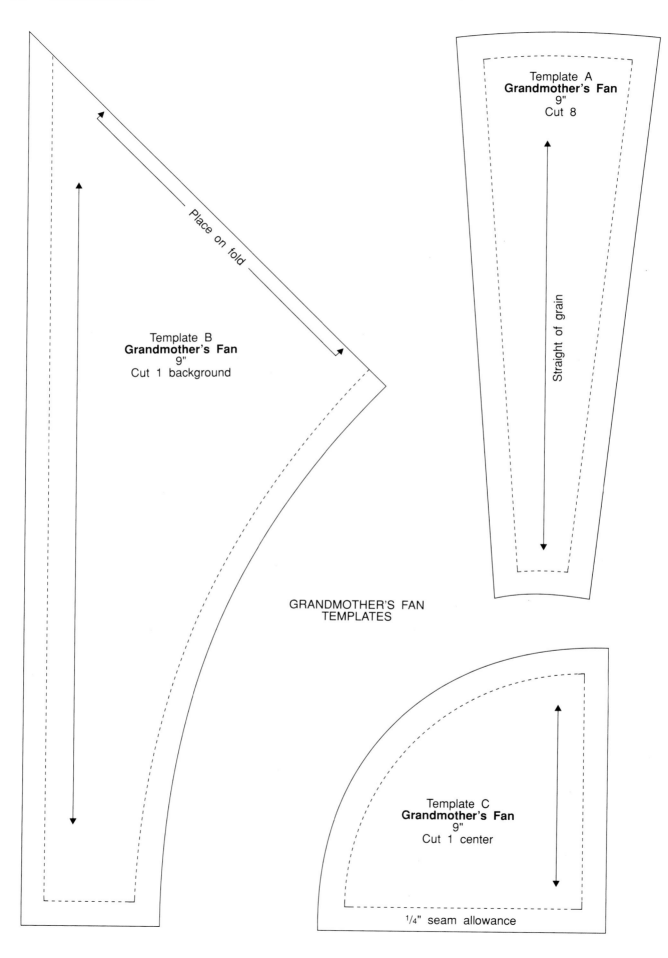

Place on fold

Template B
Grandmother's Fan
9"
Cut 1 background

Template A
Grandmother's Fan
9"
Cut 8

Straight of grain

GRANDMOTHER'S FAN
TEMPLATES

Template C
Grandmother's Fan
9"
Cut 1 center

¼" seam allowance

Log Cabin Color Study

The "Hawaiian Cabin" mixes fabulous fabrics and the easy-to-sew Log Cabin design to make this 62"-square picnic quilt by Carolyn Meerian a favorite for "almost" instant gratification.

The Log Cabin Color Study was made by using a lively print as the guide for choosing the solid colors to make a 55½"-square beach quilt.

Finished Size: *55½" x 55½"*

To create these colorful Log Cabin quilts, we started with a bright tropical print and chose a related accent in a solid color for the center of the block. We used six related solid colors for the "logs" on the solid half of the blocks and for the outer "piano key" border. Then we chose another coordinating tropical print for the inner border. "Hawaiian Cabin" (inset photo) is a variation of the Log Cabin Color Study quilt.

Materials: *44"-wide fabric*
- *⅔ yd. bright tropical print for "logs"*
- *⅛ yd. solid accent color for block centers*
- *¼ yd. each of 6 solid colors to coordinate with tropical print*
- *1 yd. coordinating tropical print for inner border*
- *Backing, batting, binding, and thread to finish*

Cutting: *All strips are cut across fabric width (crosswise grain).*
1. From the tropical print for the Log Cabin blocks, cut 8 strips, each 3" wide.
2. From the solid color for the centers of the Log Cabin blocks, cut one 3"-wide strip.
3. From each of the 6 solid colors, cut 2 strips, each 3" wide. Set aside for the "logs." Cut the remainder of each fabric into 3"-wide strips and set aside for the piano key borders.
4. From the tropical print for the inner border, cut 4 strips, each 5½" x 40½".

Directions

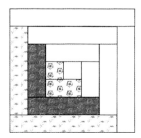

Log Cabin

1. Decide how you want to arrange the solid colors in the block and paste up a sample block for reference, giving each solid color a number.

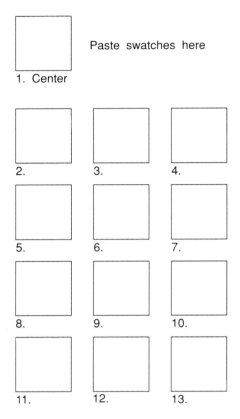

Paste swatches here

1. Center

2.   3.   4.

5.   6.   7.

8.   9.   10.

11.   12.   13.

2. Arrange the strips to the side of your sewing area in the order shown. This is the order of sewing; each solid color will be used only once in the block.

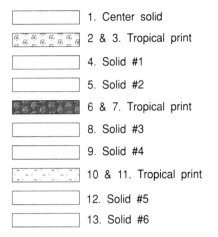

1. Center solid
2 & 3. Tropical print
4. Solid #1
5. Solid #2
6 & 7. Tropical print
8. Solid #3
9. Solid #4
10 & 11. Tropical print
12. Solid #5
13. Solid #6

3. Assemble 4 Log Cabin blocks, following the general directions for Log Cabin blocks, beginning with step 5 on page 22.

4. Join the 4 blocks into a center medallion.

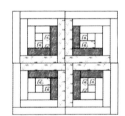

5. Add the inner border strips to the center medallion, Log Cabin fashion. Stitch the first strip to one edge of the quilt, ending stitching (temporarily) 2" from one end of quilt. Press seam toward border.

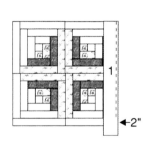

Add the second border strip to the quilt as shown. Press seam toward border.

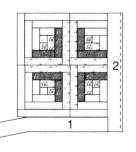

13.
Solid #6

9.
Solid #4

5.
Solid #2

10. Tropical print

6. Tropical print

2. Tropical print

1. Center Solid

4. Solid #1

8. Solid #3

12. Solid #5

3. Tropical print

7. Tropical print

11. Tropical print

Add the third and then the fourth border strip as shown and press seams toward border.

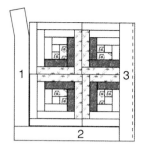 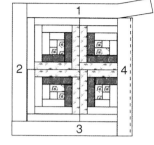

Finish the borders by stitching the unstitched section on the first strip.

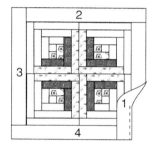

6. Stitch the remaining 3" x 44" strips of the solid-colored fabrics into random strip groupings of 5 strips each, alternating the sewing direction as each new strip is added and using scant ¼"-wide seams to avoid curving and distortion of the strip-pieced unit.

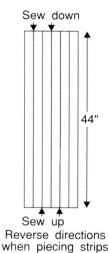

7. Crosscut the strip-pieced units into 5½" wide segments, checking to make sure that each segment is "true" before cutting. You will probably find it necessary to true up an edge of each unit as you cut, cutting away ⅛" to ¼" on one side to keep the segments squared.

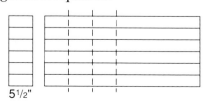

8. For each border, sew 4 piano key strip-pieced segments together to create a border strip that measures 5½" x 50¼". There should be 20 "piano keys" in each border strip. If necessary, use scant ¼"-wide seams when joining the segments into border strips to make them the correct length. Measure strips and adjust length, if necessary, by stitching slightly deeper or shallower seams, joining the keys.

9. Sew the piano key borders to the quilt, Log Cabin fashion, as shown in step 5 on page 78.

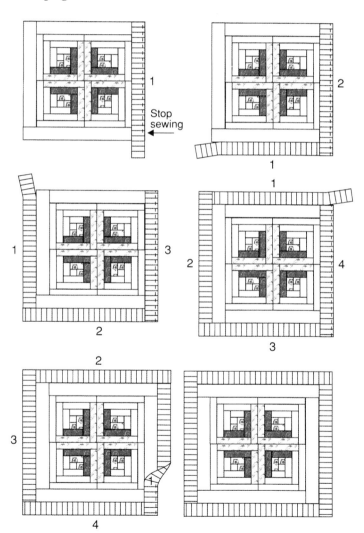

Creativity has been the fabric of Virginia Robertson's life since her childhood in rural Kansas. Her full-time venture into quiltmaking is a satisfying form of self expression, inspired by a successful show of art quilts that she created for her Master's of Fine Arts thesis. The proposal for her thesis was turned down, but her inspiration became the basis for a popular and thriving quilt shop.

After a successful university teaching career, Virginia returned to her Kansas roots and started Osage County Quilt Factory in her bedroom and garage. When the demand for her designs outgrew her space, she bought an old church and before long her studio was a quilt shop!

Today, Virginia's husband, Lynn, keeps the computers humming while her staff ably runs the shop so she can concentrate on the wholesale, mail-order and publishing aspects of the business she has built. This busy lady continues to introduce patterns and books as fast as her imagination will allow, and she designs a line of fabric specifically for quilters, too!